BECKET

Thomas Becket was Henry II's boon companion and political lieutenant, notably in the king's struggle to curb the power of the clergy. When the Archbishop of Canterbury died Henry forced Becket, much against his will, to take his place. Becket told the king: 'If I become archbishop I shall cease to be your friend,' and his first act as archbishop was to give up his mistresses and sell his horses and rich clothes. He, who with Henry had fought the Church for the good of the State, now felt responsible for the honour of God. The conflict between the king and Becket was inevitable, and was followed, just as inevitably, by murder and remorse.

'M. Anouilh's finest play since *Antigone....*'
The Times.

'It is a major play, that shows at their most confident Anouilh's great gift for story-telling and his rare sense of theatrical effect'. *Punch.*

The picture on the front cover is of Bruno Cremer as Becket and Pierre Pernet as The Little Monk in the production at the Theatre Montparnasse Gaston Baty in Paris.

BECKET

OR

The Honour of God

BY

JEAN ANOUILH

Translated by
LUCIENNE HILL

METHUEN DRAMA

A Methuen Modern Play

FIRST PUBLISHED 1961
THE PAPERBACK EDITION
FIRST PUBLISHED 1963
REPRINTED FOUR TIMES
REPRINTED 1971
REPRINTED 1974, 1977 AND 1979 BY EYRE METHUEN
REPRINTED 1982, 1984, 1986 BY METHUEN LONDON LTD
REPRINTED IN 1990 BY METHUEN DRAMA,
MICHELIN HOUSE, 81 FULHAM ROAD, LONDON SW3 6RB
ISBN 0 413 32060 X

REPRODUCED, PRINTED AND BOUND IN GREAT BRITAIN
BY COX & WYMAN LTD, READING, BERKS

Caution

This play was first produced in England by the Royal Shakespeare Theatre Company at the Aldwych Theatre on July 11, 1961, with the following cast:

KING HENRY OF ENGLAND	Christopher Plummer
THOMAS BECKET	Eric Porter
ARCHBISHOP OF CANTERBURY	Donald Layne-Smith
BISHOP OF OXFORD	P. G. Stephens
BISHOP OF YORK	Peter Russell
GILBERT FOLLIOT, *Bishop of London*	Peter Jeffrey
SAXON FATHER	Alan Downer
SAXON GIRL	Jeanne Hepple
SAXON SON	Barry MacGregor
FIRST BARON	George Murcell
SECOND BARON	Clive Swift
THIRD BARON	Edward Argent
FOURTH BARON	Roy Dotrice
GWENDOLEN	Diana Rigg
FRENCH GIRL	Marian Diamond
FIRST SOLDIER	Geoffrey Stavert
LITTLE MONK	Ian Holm
PROVOST MARSHALL	Philip Voss
SECOND SOLDIER	Stuart Hoyle
WILLIAM OF CORBEIL	Terence Greenidge
AN OFFICER	Geoffrey Stavert
SERVANTS TO BECKET	William Austin, Ian Cullen
QUEEN MOTHER	Gwen Ffrangcon-Davies
YOUNG QUEEN	Yvonne Bonnamy
PRINCES	Dane Howell, John Fox
ETIENEE, *a monk*	Barry MacGregor
FRENCH PRIEST	P. G. Stephens
FRENCH CHOIR BOY	John Fox
FIRST MONK	Edward Argent

SECOND MONK	Alan Downer
A PAGE	Philip Voss
KING LOUIS OF FRANCE	Patrick Wymark
ARUNDEL	James Keen
THE POPE	Roy Dotrice
A CARDINAL	George Murcell
A SENTRY	Alan Downer
YOUNG SENTRY	Barry MacGregor

The action takes place in England and France during the reign of King Henry II of England.

Directed by Peter Hall.

ACT ONE

An indeterminate set, with pillars, We are in the cathedral.
Centre stage: BECKET'S *tomb, a stone slab with a name*
carved on it. Two SENTRIES *come in and take up their*
position upstage. Then the KING *enters from the back.*
He is wearing his crown, and is naked under a big cloak.
A PAGE *follows at a distance. The* KING *hesitates a*
moment before the tomb, then removes his cloak with a
swift movement and the PAGE *takes it away. He falls to*
his knees on the stone floor and prays, alone, naked, in
the middle of the stage. Behind the pillars, in the shadows,
one senses the disquieting presence of unseen lookers-on.

KING. Well, Thomas Becket, are you satisfied? I am naked
at your tomb and your monks are coming to flog me. What
an end to our story! You, rotting in this tomb, larded with
my baron's dagger thrusts, and I, naked, shivering in the
draught, and waiting like an idiot for those brutes to
come and thrash me. Don't you think we'd have done
better to understand each other?

> BECKET *in his Archbishop's robes, just as he was on the*
> *day of his death, has appeared on the side of the stage,*
> *from behind a pillar. He says softly:*

BECKET. Understand each other? It wasn't possible.
KING. I said 'In all save the honour of the realm'. It was
you who taught me that slogan, after all.
BECKET. I answered you 'All save the honour of God'. We
were like two deaf men talking.

KING. How cold it was on that bare plain at La Ferté-Bernard, the last time we two met! It's funny, it's always been cold, in our story. Save at the beginning, when we were friends. We had a few fine summer evenings together, with the girls ... (*He says suddenly.*) Did you love Gwendolen, Archbishop? Did you hate me, that night when I said 'I am the king', and took her from you? Perhaps that's what you never could forgive me for?

BECKET (*quietly*). I've forgotten.

KING. Yet we were like two brothers, weren't we – you and I? That night it was a childish prank – a lusty lad shouting 'I am the king!' ... I was so young. ... And every thought in my head came from you, you know that.

BECKET (*gently, as if to a little boy*). Pray, Henry, and don't talk so much.

KING (*irritably*). If you think I'm in the mood for praying at the moment. ...

> BECKET *quietly withdraws into the darkness and disappears during the* KING'S *next speech.*

I can see them through my fingers, spying on me from the aisles. Say what you like, they're an oafish lot, those Saxons of yours! To give oneself over naked to those ruffians! With my delicate skin. ... Even you'd be afraid. Besides, I'm ashamed. Ashamed of this whole masquerade. I need them, though, that's the trouble. I have to rally them to my cause, against my son, who'll gobble up my kingdom if I let him. So I've come to make my peace with their Saint. You must admit it's funny. You've become a Saint, and here am I, the King, desperately in need of that great amorphous mass which could do nothing, up till now, save lie inert beneath its own enormous weight, cowering under blows, and which is all-powerful now. What use are conquests, when you stop to think? They

6

are England now, because of their vast numbers, and the rate at which they breed – like rabbits, to make good the massacres. But one must always pay the price – that's another thing you taught me, Thomas Becket, when you were still advising me. ... You taught me everything. ... (*Dreamily.*) Ah, those were happy times. ... At the peep of dawn – well, our dawn that is, around noon, because we always went to bed very late – you'd come into my room, as I was emerging from the bathhouse, rested, smiling, debonair, as fresh as if we'd never spent the entire night drinking and whoring through the town. (*He says, a little sourly.*) That's another thing you were better at than me. ...

The PAGE *has come in. He wraps a white towel round the* KING *and proceeds to rub him down. Offstage is heard for the first time – we will hear it often – the gay, ironical Scottish marching song which* BECKET *is always whistling.*

The lighting changes. We are still in the empty cathedral.

Then, a moment or so later, BECKET *will draw aside a curtain and reveal the* KING'S *room. Their manner, his and the* KING'S, *faraway at first, like a memory relived, will gradually become more real.*

THOMAS BECKET, *dressed as a nobleman, elegant, young, charming, in his short doublet and pointed, upturned shoes, comes in blithely and greets the* KING.

BECKET.   My respects, my Lord!
KING (*his face brightening*).   Oh, Thomas ... I thought you were still asleep.
BECKET.   I've already been for a short gallop to Richmond and back, my Lord. There's a divine nip in the air.

KING (*his teeth chattering*).   To think you actually like the cold! (*To the* PAGE.) Rub harder, pig!

> Smiling, BECKET *pushes the* PAGE *aside and proceeds to rub the* KING *himself.*

(*To the* PAGE.) Throw a log on the fire and get out. Come back and dress me later.

BECKET.   My prince, I shall dress you myself.

> *The* PAGE *goes.*

KING.   Nobody rubs me down the way you do. Thomas, what would I do without you? You're a nobleman, why do you play at being my valet? If I asked my barons to do this, they'd start a civil war!

BECKET (*smiling*).   They'll come round to it in time, when Kings have learnt to play their role. I am your servant, my prince, that's all. Helping you to govern or helping you get warm again is part of the same thing to me. I like helping you.

KING (*with an affectionate little gesture*).   My little Saxon! At the beginning, when I told them I was taking you into my service, do you know what they all said? They said you'd seize the chance to knife me in the back one day.

BECKET (*smiling as he dresses him*).   Did you believe them, my prince?

KING.   N . . . no. I was a bit scared at first. You know I scare easily. . . . But you looked so well brought up, beside those brutes. However did you come to speak French without a trace of an English accent?

BECKET.   My parents were able to keep their lands by agreeing to 'collaborate', as they say, with the King your father. They sent me to France as a boy to acquire a good French accent.

KING.   To France? Not to Normandy?

8

BECKET (*still smiling*). That was their one patriotic conceit. They loathed the Norman accent.

KING (*distinctly*). Only the accent?

BECKET (*lightly and inscrutably*). My father was a very severe man. I would never have taken the liberty of questioning him on his personal convictions while he was alive. And his death shed no light on them, naturally. He managed, by collaborating, to amass a considerable fortune. As he was also a man of rigid principles, I imagine he contrived to do it in accordance with his conscience. That's a little piece of sleight of hand that men of principle are very skilful at in troubled times.

KING. And you?

BECKET (*feigning not to understand the question*). I, my Lord?

KING (*putting a touch of contempt into his voice, for despite his admiration for* THOMAS, *or perhaps because of it, he would like to score a point against him occasionally*). The sleight of hand, were you adept at it too?

BECKET (*still smiling*). Mine was a different problem. I was a frivolous man, you'll agree? In fact, it never came up at all. I adore hunting and only the Normans and their protégés had the right to hunt. I adore luxury and luxury was Norman. I adore life and the Saxons' only birthright was slaughter. I'll add that I adore honour.

KING (*with faint surprise*). And was honour reconciled with collaboration too?

BECKET (*lightly*). I had the right to draw my sword against the first Norman nobleman who tried to lay hands on my sister. I killed him in single combat. It's a detail, but it has its points.

KING (*a little slyly*). You could always have slit his throat and fled into the forest, as so many did.

BECKET. That would have been uncomfortable, and not a

9

lot of use. My sister would immediately have been raped by some other Norman baron, like all the Saxon girls. Today, she is respected. (*Lightly*.) My Lord, did I tell you? – My new gold dishes have arrived from Florence. Will my Liege do me the honour of christening them with me at my house?

KING. Gold dishes! You lunatic!

BECKET. I'm setting a new fashion.

KING. I'm your King and I eat off silver!

BECKET. My prince, your expenses are heavy and I have only my pleasures to pay for. The trouble is I'm told they scratch easily. Still, we'll see. I received two forks as well —

KING. Forks?

BECKET. Yes. It's a new instrument, a devilish little thing to look at – and to use too. It's for pronging meat and carrying it to your mouth. It saves you dirtying your fingers.

KING. But then you dirty the fork?

BECKET. Yes. But it's washable.

KING. So are your fingers. I don't see the point.

BECKET. It hasn't any, practically speaking. But it's refined, it's subtle. It's very un-Norman.

KING (*with sudden delight*). You must order me a dozen! I want to see my great fat baron's faces, at the first court banquet, when I present them with that! We won't tell them what they're for. We'll have no end of fun with them.

BECKET (*laughing*). A dozen! Easy now, my Lord! Forks are very expensive, you know! My prince, it's time for the Privy Council.

KING (*laughing too*). They won't make head nor tail of them! I bet you they'll think they're a new kind of dagger. We'll have a hilarious time!

They go out, laughing, behind the curtain, which draws apart to reveal the same set, with the pillars. The Council Chamber. The COUNCILLORS *stand waiting. The* KING *and* BECKET *come in, still laughing.*

KING (*sitting in a chair*).   Gentlemen, the Council is open. I have summoned you here today to deal with this refusal of the clergy to pay the absentee tax. We really must come to an understanding about who rules this kingdom, the Church (*The* ARCHBISHOP *tries to speak.*) – just a moment, Archbishop! – or me! But before we quarrel, let us take the good news first. I have decided to revive the office of Chancellor of England, keeper of the Triple Lion Seal, and to entrust it to my loyal servant and subject, Thomas Becket.

> BECKET *rises in surprise, the colour draining from his face.*

BECKET.   My Lord! . . .

KING (*roguishly*).   What's the matter, Becket? Do you want to go and piss already? True, we both had gallons to drink last night! (*He looks at him with delight.*) Well, that's good! I've managed to surprise you for once, little Saxon.

BECKET (*dropping on one knee, says gravely*).   My Liege, this is a token of your confidence of which I fear I may not be worthy. I am very young, frivolous perhaps —

KING.   I'm young too. And you know more than all of us put together. (*To the others.*) He's read books, you know. It's amazing the amount he knows. He'll checkmate the lot of you! Even the Archbishop! As for his frivolity, don't let him fool you! He drinks strong wine, he likes to enjoy himself, but he's a lad who thinks every minute of the time! Sometimes it embarrasses me to feel him

11

thinking away beside me. Get up, Thomas. I never did anything without your advice, anyway. Nobody knew it, now everybody will, that's all. (*He bursts out laughing, pulls something out of his pocket and gives it to* BECKET.) There. That's the Seal. Don't lose it. Without the Seal, there's no more England and we'll all have to go back to Normandy, Now, to work!

The ARCHBISHOP *rises, all smiles, now the first shock is over.*

ARCHBISHOP. May I crave permission to salute, with my Lord's approval, my young and learned archdeacon here? For I was the first – I am weak enough to be proud of pointing it out – to notice him and take him under my wing. The presence at this Council, with the preponderant title of Chancellor of England, of one of our brethren – our spiritual son in a sense – is a guarantee for the Church of this country that a new era of agreement and mutual understanding is dawning for us all, and we must now, in a spirit of confident co-operation . . .

KING (*interrupting*). Etc, etc. . . . Thank you, Archbishop! I knew this nomination would please you. But don't rely too much on Becket to play your game. He is my man. (*He turns to* BECKET, *beaming*.) Come to think of it, I'd forgotten you were a deacon, little Saxon.

BECKET (*smiling*). So had I, my prince.

KING. Tell me – I'm not talking about wenching, that's a venial sin – but on the odd occasions when I've seen you fighting it seems to me you have a mighty powerful sword arm for a priest! How do you reconcile that with the Church's commandment forbidding a priest to shed blood?

OXFORD (*prudently*). Our young friend is only a deacon, he has not yet taken all his vows, my Lord. The Church

12

in its wisdom knows that youth must have its day and that under the sacred pretext of a war – a holy war, I mean, of course – young men are permitted to —

KING (*interrupting*). All wars are holy wars, Bishop! I defy you to find me a serious belligerent who doesn't have Heaven on his side, in theory. Let's get back to the point.

ARCHBISHOP. By all means, your Highness.

KING. Our customs demand that every landowner with sufficient acreage to maintain one must send a man at arms to the quarterly review of troops, fully armed and shield in hand, or pay a tax in silver. Where is my tax?

OXFORD. *Distinguo*, your Highness.

KING. Distinguish as much as you like. I've made up my mind. I want my money. My purse is open, just drop it in. (*He sprawls back in his chair and picks his teeth. To* BECKET.) Thomas, I don't know about you, but I'm starving. Have them bring us something to eat.

> BECKET *makes a sign to the* SENTRY *who goes out. A pause. The* ARCHBISHOP *rises.*

ARCHBISHOP. A layman who shirks his duty to the State, which is to assist his Prince with arms, should pay the tax. Nobody will question that.

KING (*jovially*). Least of all the clergy!

ARCHBISHOP (*continuing*). A churchman's duty to the State is to assist his Prince in his prayers, and in his educational and charitable enterprises. He cannot therefore be liable to such a tax unless he neglects those duties.

OXFORD. Have we refused to pray?

KING (*rising in fury*). Gentlemen! Do you seriously think that I am going to let myself be swindled out of more than two-thirds of my revenues with arguments of that sort?

In the days of the Conquest, when there was booty to be had, our Norman abbots tucked up their robes all right. And lustily too! Sword in fist, hams in the saddle, at cockcrow or earlier! 'Let's go to it, Sire! Out with the Saxon scum! It's God's will! It's God's will!' You had to hold them back then! And on the odd occasions when you wanted a little mass, they never had the time. They'd mislaid their vestments, the churches weren't equipped – any excuse to put it off, for fear they'd miss some of the pickings while their backs were turned!

ARCHBISHOP. Those heroic days are over. It is peace-time now.

KING. Then pay up! I won't budge from that. (*Turning to* BECKET.) Come on, Chancellor, say something! Has your new title caught your tongue?

BECKET. May I respectfully draw my Lord Archbishop's attention to one small point?

KING (*grunting*). Respectfully, but firmly. You're the Chancellor now.

BECKET (*calmly and casually*). England is a ship.

KING (*beaming*). Why, that's neat! We must use that, some time.

BECKET. In the hazards of sea-faring, the instinct of self-preservation has always told men that there must be one and only one master on board ship. Mutinous crews who drown their captain always end up, after a short interval of anarchy, by entrusting themselves body and soul to one of their number, who then proceeds to rule over them, more harshly sometimes than their drowned captain.

ARCHBISHOP. My Lord Chancellor – my young friend – there is in fact a saying – the captain is sole master after God. (*He thunders suddenly, with a voice one did not suspect from that frail body.*) After God!

14

He crosses himself. All the BISHOPS *follow suit. The wind of excommunication shivers through the Council. The* KING, *awed, crosses himself too and mumbles, a little cravenly:*

KING. Nobody's trying to question God's authority, Archbishop.

BECKET (*who alone has remained unperturbed*). God steers the ship by inspiring the captain's decisions. But I never heard tell that He gave His instructions directly to the helmsman.

GILBERT FOLLIOT, BISHOP OF LONDÓN, *rises. He is a thin-lipped, venomous man.*

FOLLIOT. Our young Chancellor is only a deacon – but he is a member of the Church. The few years he has spent out in the tumult of the world cannot have made him forget so soon that it is through His Church Militant and more particularly through the intermediaries of our Holy Father the Pope and his Bishops – his qualified representatives – that God dictates His decisions to men!

BECKET. There is a chaplain on board every ship, but he is not required to determine the size of the crew's rations, nor to take the vessel's bearings. My Reverend Lord the Bishop of London – who is the grandson of a sailor, they tell me – cannot have forgotten that point either.

FOLLIOT (*yelping*). I will not allow personal insinuations to compromise the dignity of a debate of this importance! The integrity and honour of the Church of England are at stake!

KING (*cheerfully*). No big words, Bishop. You know as well as I do that all that's at stake is its money. I need money for my wars. Will the Church give me any, yes or no?

ARCHBISHOP (*cautiously*). The Church of England has always acknowledged that it was its duty to assist the King, to the best of its ability, in all his needs.

KING. There's a fine speech. But I don't like the past tense, Archbishop. There's something so nostalgic about it. I like the present. And the future. Are you going to pay up?

ARCHBISHOP. Your Highness, I am here to defend the privileges which your illustrious forefather, William, granted to the Church of England. Would you have the heart to tamper with your forefather's work?

KING. May he rest in peace. His work is inviolable. But where he is now he doesn't need money. I'm still on earth, unfortunately, and I do.

FOLLIOT. Your Highness, this is a question of principle!

KING. I'm levying troops, Bishop! I have sent for fifteen hundred German foot soldiers and three thousand Swiss infantry to help fight the King of France. And nobody has ever paid the Swiss with principles.

BECKET (*rises suddenly and says incisively*). I think, your Highness, that it is pointless to pursue a discussion in which neither speaker is listening to the other. The law and custom of the land give us the means of coercion. We will use them.

FOLLIOT (*beside himself*). Would you dare – you whom she raised from the obscurity of your base origins – to plunge a dagger in the bosom of your Mother Church?

BECKET. My Lord and King has given me his seal with the Three Lions to guard. My mother is England now.

FOLLIOT (*frothing, and slightly ridiculous*). A deacon! A miserable deacon nourished in our bosom! Traitor! Little viper! Libertine! Sycophant! Saxon!

KING. My reverend friend, I suggest you respect my Chancellor, or else I'll call my guards.

*He has raised his voice a little towards the end of this
speech. The* GUARDS *come in.*

(*Surprised.*) Why, here they are! Oh, no, it's my snack.
Excuse me, gentlemen, but around noon I need something to peck at or I tend to feel weak. And a King has
no right to weaken, I needn't tell you that. I'll have it in
my chapel, then I can pray directly afterwards. Come and
sit with me, son.

He goes out, taking BECKET *with him. The three*
BISHOPS *have risen, deeply offended. They move
away, murmuring to one another, with sidelong glances
in the direction in which the* KING *went out.*

FOLLIOT.   We must appeal to Rome! We must take a firm
line!

YORK.   My Lord Archbishop, you are the Primate of
England. Your person is inviolate and your decisions on
all matters affecting the Church are law in this country.
You have a weapon against such intransigence: excommunication.

OXFORD.   We must not use it save with a great deal of
prudence, Reverend Bishop. The Church has always
triumphed over the centuries, but it has triumphed
prudently. Let us bide our time. The King's rages are
terrible, but they don't last. They are fires of straw.

FOLLIOT.   The little self-seeker he has at his elbow now
will make it his business to kindle them. And I think, like
the Reverend Bishop, that only the excommunication of
that young libertine can reduce him to impotence.

BECKET *comes in.*

BECKET.   My Lords, the King has decided to adjourn his
Privy Council. He thinks that a night of meditation will

17

inspire your Lordships with a wise and equitable solution – which he authorizes you to come and submit to him tomorrow.

FOLLIOT (*with a bitter laugh*). You mean it's time for the hunt.

BECKET (*smiling*). Yes, my Lord Bishop, to be perfectly frank with you, it is. Believe me, I am personally most grieved at this difference of opinion and the brutal form it has taken. But I cannot go back on what I said as Chancellor of England. We are all bound, laymen as well as priests, by the same feudal oath we took to the King as our Lord and Sovereign; the oath to preserve his life, limbs, dignity and honour. None of you, I think, has forgotten the words of that oath?

ARCHBISHOP (*quietly*). We have not forgotten it, my son. No more than the other oath we took, before that – the oath to God. You are young, and still uncertain of yourself, perhaps. Yet you have, in those few words, taken a resolution the meaning of which has not escaped me. Will you allow an old man, who is very close to death, and who, in this rather sordid argument, was defending more perhaps than you suspect – to hope, as a father, that you will never know the bitterness of realizing, one day, that you made a mistake. (*He holds out his ring and* BECKET *kisses it.*) I give you my blessing, my son.

BECKET *has knelt. Now he rises and says lightly:*

BECKET. An unworthy son, Father, alas. But when is one worthy? And worthy of what?

He pirouettes and goes out, insolent and graceful as a young boy.

FOLLIOT (*violently*). Such insults to your Grace cannot be tolerated! This young rake's impudence must be crushed!

18

ARCHBISHOP (*thoughtfully*).   He was with me for a long time. His is a strange, elusive nature. Don't imagine he is the ordinary libertine that outward appearances would suggest. I've had plenty of opportunity to observe him, in the bustle of pleasure and daily living. He is, as it were, detached. As if seeking his real self.

FOLLIOT.   Break him, my Lord, before he finds it! Or the clergy of this country will pay dearly.

ARCHBISHOP.   We must be very circumspect. It is our task to see into the hearts of men. And I am not sure that this one will always be our enemy.

The ARCHBISHOP *and the three* BISHOPS *go out. The* KING *is heard calling offstage:*

KING.   Well, son, have they gone? Are you coming hunting?

Trees come down from the flies. The black velvet curtain at the back opens on a clear sky, transforming the pillars into the leafless trees of a forest in winter. Bugles. The lights have gone down. When they go up again, the KING *and* BECKET *are on horseback, each with a hawk on his gauntleted wrist. Torrential rain is heard.*

KING.   Here comes the deluge. (*Unexpectedly.*) Do you like hunting this way, with hawks?

BECKET.   I don't much care to delegate my errands; I prefer to feel a wild boar on the end of my spear. When he turns and charges there's a moment of delicious personal contact when one feels, at last, responsible for oneself.

KING.   It's odd, this craving for danger. Why are you all so hell bent on risking your necks for the most futile reasons?

19

BECKET. One has to gamble with one's life to feel alive.

KING. Or dead! You make me laugh. (*To his hawk*.) Quiet, my pretty, quiet! We'll take your hood off in a minute. You couldn't give much of a performance under all these trees. I'll tell you one creature that loves hawking, anyway, and that's a hawk! It seems to me we've rubbed our backsides sore with three hours' riding, just to give them this royal pleasure.

BECKET (*smiling*). My Lord, these are Norman hawks. They belong to the master race. They have a right to it.

KING (*suddenly, as he reins his horse*). Do you love me, Becket?

BECKET. I am your servant, my prince.

KING. Did you love me when I made you Chancellor? I wonder sometimes if you're capable of love. Do you love Gwendolen?

BECKET. She is my mistress, my prince.

KING. Why do you put labels on to everything to justify your feelings?

BECKET. Because, without labels, the world would have no shape, my prince.

KING. Is it so important for the world to have a shape?

BECKET. It's essential, my prince, otherwise we can't know what we're doing.(*Bugles in the distance*.) The rain is getting heavier, my Lord! Come, let us shelter in that hut over there.

> *He gallops off. After a second of confused indecision, the* KING *gallops after him, holding his hawk high and shouting:*

KING. Becket! You didn't answer my question!

> *He disappears into the forest. Bugles again. The four* BARONS *cross the stage, galloping after them, and vanish into the forest. Thunder. Lightning. A hut has*

appeared to one side of the stage. BECKET *is heard shouting:*

BECKET.   Hey there! You! Fellow! Can we put the horses under cover in your barn? Do you know how to rub down a horse? And have a look at the right forefoot of messire's horse. I think the shoe is loose. We'll sit out the storm under your roof.

After a second, the KING *enters the hut, followed by a hairy* SAXON PEASANT *who, cap in hand, bows repeatedly, in terrified silence.*

KING (*shaking himself*).   What a soaking! I'll catch my death! (*He sneezes.*) All this just to keep the hawks amused! (*Shouting at the man.*) What are you waiting for? Light a fire, dog! It's freezing cold in this shack. (*The* MAN, *terror-stricken, does not move. The* KING *sneezes again. To* BECKET.) What is he waiting for?

BECKET.   Wood is scarce, my Lord, I don't suppose he has any left.

KING.   What – in the middle of the forest?

BECKET.   They are entitled to two measures of dead wood. One branch more and they're hanged.

KING (*astounded*).   Really? And yet people are always complaining about the amount of dead wood in the forests. Still, that's a problem for my intendants, not me. (*Shouting at the* MAN.) Run and pick up all the wood you can carry and build us a roaring fire! We won't hang you this time, dog!

The MAN, *terrified, dares not obey.* BECKET *says gently:*

BECKET.   Go, my son. Your King commands it. You've the right.

21

The MAN *goes out, trembling and bowing to the ground repeatedly.*

KING.   Why do you call that old man your son?

BECKET.   Why not? You call him dog, my prince.

KING.   It's a manner of speaking. Saxons are always called 'dog'. I can't think why, really. One could just as well have called them 'Saxon'! But that smelly old rag-bag your son! (*Sniffing.*) What on earth can they eat to make the place stink so – dung?

BECKET.   Turnips.

KING.   Turnips – what are they?

BECKET.   Roots.

KING (*amused*).   Do they eat roots?

BECKET.   Those who live in the forests can't grow anything else.

KING.   Why don't they move out into the open country then?

BECKET.   They would be hanged if they left their area.

KING.   Oh, I see. Mark you, that must make life a lot simpler, if you know you'll be hanged at the least show of initiative. You must ask yourself far fewer questions. They don't know their luck! But still you haven't told me why you called the fellow your son?

BECKET (*lightly*).   My prince, he is so poor and so bereft and I am so strong beside him, that he really is my son.

KING.   We'd go a long way with that theory!

BECKET.   Besides, my prince, you're appreciably younger than I am and you call me 'son' sometimes.

KING.   That's got nothing to do with it. It's because I love you.

BECKET.   You are our King. We are all your sons and in your hands.

KING.   What, Saxons too?

BECKET (*lightly, as he strips off his gloves*).   England will be fully built, my prince, on the day the Saxons are your sons as well.

KING.   You are a bore today! I get the feeling that I'm listening to the Archbishop. And I'm dying of thirst. Hunt around and see if you can't find us something to drink. Go on, it's your son's house!

> BECKET *starts looking, and leaves the room after a while. The* KING *looks around too, examining the hut with curiosity, touches things with grimaces of distaste. Suddenly he notices a kind of trapdoor at the foot of a wall. He opens it, thrusts his hand in and pulls out a terrified* GIRL. *He shouts:*

Hey, Thomas! Thomas!

> BECKET *comes in.*

BECKET.   Have you found something to drink, my Lord?

KING (*holding the* GIRL *at arm's length*).   No. Something to eat. What do you say to that, if it's cleaned up a bit?

BECKET (*coldly*).   She's pretty.

KING.   She stinks a bit, but we could wash her. Look, did you ever see anything so tiny? How old would you say it was – fifteen, sixteen?

BECKET (*quietly*).   It can talk, my Lord. (*Gently, to the* GIRL.) How old are you?

> *The* GIRL *looks at them in terror and says nothing.*

KING.   You see? Of course it can't talk!

> *The* MAN *has come back with the wood, and stops in the doorway, terrified.*

How old is your daughter, dog?

The MAN *trembles like a cornered animal and says nothing.*

He's dumb as well, that son of yours. How did you get him – with a deaf girl? It's funny the amount of dumb people I meet the second I set foot out of my palace. I rule over a kingdom of the dumb. Can you tell me why?

BECKET. They're afraid, my prince.

KING. I know that. And a good thing too. The populace must live in fear; it's essential. The moment they stop being afraid they have only one thought in mind – to frighten other people instead. And they adore doing that! Just as much as we do! Give them a chance to do it and they catch up fast, those sons of yours! Did you never see a peasants' revolt? I did once, in my father's reign, when I was a child. It's not a pretty sight. (*He looks at the* MAN, *exasperated.*) Look at it, will you? It's tongue-tied, it's obtuse, it stinks and the country is crawling with them! (*He seizes the* GIRL, *who was trying to run away.*) Stay here, you! (*To* BECKET.) I ask you, what use is it?

BECKET (*smiling*). It scratches the soil, it makes bread.

KING. Pooh, the English eat so little of it. . . . At the French court, yes, I dare say – they fairly stuff it down! But here!

BECKET (*smiling*). The troops have to be fed. For a King without troops. . . .

KING (*struck by this*). True enough! Yes, that makes sense. There must be some sort of reason in all these absurdities. Well, well, you little Saxon philosopher, you! I don't know how you do it, but you'll turn me into an intelligent man yet! The odd thing is, it's so ugly and yet it makes such pretty daughters. How do you explain that, you who can explain it all?

BECKET. At twenty, before he lost his teeth and took on

that indeterminate age the common people have, that man may have been handsome. He may have had one night of love, one minute when he too was a king, and shed his fear. Afterwards, his pauper's life went on, eternally the same. And he and his wife no doubt forgot it all. But the seed was sown.

KING (*dreamily*). You have such a way of telling things. ... (*He looks at the* GIRL.) Do you think she'll grow ugly too?

BECKET. For sure.

KING. If we made her a whore and kept her at the palace, would she stay pretty?

BECKET. Perhaps.

KING. Then we'd be doing her a service, don't you think?

BECKET (*coldly*). No doubt.

The MAN *stiffens. The* GIRL *cowers in terror. The* BROTHER *comes in, sombre-faced, silent, threatening.*

KING. Would you believe it? They understand every word, you know! Who's that one there?

BECKET (*taking in the situation at a glance*). The brother.

KING. How do you know?

BECKET. Instinct, my Lord. (*His hand moves to his dagger.*)

KING (*bawling suddenly*). Why are they staring at me like that? I've had enough of this! I told you to get something to drink, dog!

Terrified, the MAN *scuttles off.*

BECKET. Their water will be brackish. I have a gourd of juniper-juice in my saddle-bag. (*To the* BROTHER.) Come and give me a hand, you! My horse is restive.

He seizes the BOY *roughly by the arm and hustles him*

25

out into the forest, carelessly whistling his little march-
ing song. Then, all of a sudden, he hurls himself on to
the BOY. *A short silent struggle.* BECKET *gets his knife*
away. The BOY *escapes into the forest.* BECKET
watches him go for a second, holding his wounded
hand. Then he walks round the back of the hut. The
KING *has settled himself on a bench, with his feet up*
on another, whistling to himself. He lifts the GIRL'S
skirts with his cane and examines her at leisure.

KING (*in a murmur*). All my sons! . . . (*He shakes himself.*)
That Becket! He wears me out. He keeps making me
think! I'm sure it's bad for the health. (*He gets up.*
BECKET *comes in, followed by the* MAN.) What about
that water? How much longer do I have to wait?

BECKET. Here it is, my Lord. But it's muddy. Have some
of this juniper-juice instead.

KING. Drink with me. (*He notices* BECKET'S *hand,
wrapped in a bloodstained cloth.*) What's the matter?
You're wounded!

BECKET (*hiding his hand*). No doubt about it, that horse
of mine is a nervous brute. He can't bear his saddle
touched. He bit me.

KING (*with a hearty, delighted laugh*). That's funny! Oh,
that's very funny! Milord is the best rider in the kingdom!
Milord can never find a stallion with enough spirit for
him! Milord makes us all look silly at the jousts, with his
fancy horsemanship, and when he goes to open his saddle-
bags he gets himself bitten! Like a page! (*He is almost
savagely gleeful. Then, suddenly, his gaze softens.*) You're
white as a sheet, little Saxon. . . . Why do I love you? . . .
It's funny, I don't like to think of you in pain. Show me
that hand. A horse bite can turn nasty. I'll put some of
that juniper gin on it.

26

BECKET (*snatching his hand away*). I already have, my Lord. It's nothing.

KING. Then why do you look so pale? Show me your hand.

BECKET (*with sudden coldness*). It's an ugly wound and you know you hate the sight of blood.

KING (*steps back a little, then exclaims with delight*). All this just to fetch me a drink! Wounded in the service of the King! We'll tell the others you defended me against a wild boar and I'll present you with a handsome gift this evening. What would you like?

BECKET (*softly*). This girl. (*He adds, after a pause.*) I fancy her.

A pause.

KING (*his face clouding over*). That's tiresome of you. I fancy her too. And where that's concerned, friendship goes by the board. (*A pause. His face takes on a cunning look.*) All right, then. But favour for favour. You won't forget, will you?

BECKET. No, my prince.

KING. Favour for favour; do you give me your word as a gentleman?

BECKET. Yes, my prince.

KING (*draining his glass, suddenly cheerful*). Done! She's yours. Do we take her with us or shall we have her sent?

BECKET. I'll send two soldiers to fetch her. Listen. The others have caught up.

A troop of MEN AT ARMS *have come riding up behind the shack during the end of the scene.*

KING (*to the* MAN). Wash your daughter, dog, and kill her fleas. She's going to the palace. For Milord here, who's a Saxon too. You're pleased about that, I hope? (*To*

27

BECKET *as he goes.*) Give him a gold piece. I'm feeling generous this morning.

He goes out. The MAN *looks at* BECKET *in terror.*

BECKET.   No one will come and take your daughter away. Keep her better hidden in future. And tell your son to join the others in the forest; he'll be safer there, now. I think one of the soldiers saw us. Here!

He throws him a purse and goes out. When he has gone, the MAN *snatches up the purse, then spits venomously, his face twisted with hate.*

MAN.   God rot your guts! Pig!

GIRL (*unexpectedly*).   He was handsome, that one. Is it true he's taking me to the palace?

MAN.   You whore! You Norman's trollop!

He hurls himself on to her and beats her savagely.

The KING, BECKET *and the* BARONS *have galloped off, amid the sound of bugles. The hut and the forest back-cloth disappear. We are in* BECKET'S *palace.*

FOOTMEN *push on a kind of low bed-couch, with cushions and some stools. Upstage, between two pillars, a curtain behind which can be seen the shadows of banqueting guests. Singing and roars of laughter. Downstage, curled up on the bed,* GWENDOLEN *is playing a stringed instrument. The curtain is drawn aside.* BECKET *appears. He goes to* GWENDOLEN *while the banqueting and the laughter, punctuated by hoarse, incoherent snatches of song, go on upstage.* GWENDOLEN *stops playing.*

GWENDOLEN.   Are they still eating?

BECKET.   Yes. They have an unimaginable capacity for absorbing food.

28

GWENDOLEN (*softly, beginning to play again*). How can my Lord spend his days and a large part of his nights with such creatures?

BECKET (*crouching at her feet and caressing her*). If he spent his time with learned clerics debating the sex of angels, your Lord would be even more bored, my kitten. They are as far from the true knowledge of things as mindless brutes.

GWENDOLEN (*gently, as she plays*). I don't always understand everything my Lord condescends to say to me. . . . .What I do know is that it is always very late when he comes to see me.

BECKET (*caressing her*). The only thing I love is coming to you. Beauty is one of the few things which don't shake one's faith in God.

GWENDOLEN. I am my Lord's war captive and I belong to him body and soul. God has willed it so, since He gave the Normans victory over my people. If the Welsh had won the war I would have married a man of my own race, at my father's castle. God did not will it so.

BECKET (*quietly*). That belief will do as well as any, my kitten. But, as I belong to a conquered race myself, I have a feeling that God's system is a little muddled. Go on playing.

> GWENDOLEN *starts to play again. Then she says suddenly.*

GWENDOLEN. I'm lying. You are my Lord, God or no God. And if the Welsh had been victorious, you could just as easily have stolen me from my father's castle. I should have come with you.

> *She says this gravely.* BECKET *rises abruptly and moves away.* GWENDOLEN *looks up at him with anguished eyes and stops playing.*

29

Did I say something wrong? What is the matter with my Lord?

BECKET. Nothing I don't like being loved. I told you that.

The curtain opens. The KING *appears.*

KING (*a little drunk*). Well, son, have you deserted us? It worked! I told you! They've tumbled to it! They're fighting with your forks! They've at last discovered that they're for poking one another's eyes out. They think it's a most ingenious little invention. You'd better go in, son, they'll break them in a minute.

    BECKET *goes behind the curtain to quieten his guests. He can be heard shouting:*

BECKET. Gentlemen, gentlemen! No, no, they aren't little daggers. No, truly – they're for pronging meat.... Look, let me show you again.

    Huge roars of laughter behind the curtain. The KING *has moved over to* GWENDOLEN. *He stares at her.*

KING. Was that you playing, while we were at table?
GWENDOLEN (*with a deep curtsey*). Yes, my Lord.
KING. You have every kind of accomplishment, haven't you? Get up.

    He lifts her to her feet, caressing her as he does so. She moves away, ill at ease. He says, with a wicked smile:

KING. Have I frightened you, my heart? We'll soon put that right. (*He pulls the curtain aside.*) Hey there, Becket! That's enough horseplay, my fat lads! Come and hear a little music. When the belly's full, it's good to elevate the mind a bit. (*To* GWENDOLEN.) Play!

30

The four BARONS, *bloated with food and drink, come in with* BECKET. GWENDOLEN *has taken up her instrument again. The* KING *sprawls on the bed, behind her. The* BARONS, *with much sighing and puffing, unclasp their belts and sit down on stools, where they soon fall into a stupor.* BECKET *remains standing.*

Tell her to sing us something sad. I like sad music after dinner, it helps the digestion. (*He hiccups.*) You always feed us far too well, Thomas. Where did you steal that cook of yours?

BECKET. I bought him, Sire. He's a Frenchman.

KING. Really? Aren't you afraid he might poison you? Tell me, how much does one pay for a French cook?

BECKET. A good one, like him, costs almost as much as a horse, my Lord.

KING (*genuinely outraged*). It's outrageous! What is the country coming to! No man is worth a horse! If I said 'favour for favour' – remember? – and I asked you to give him to me, would you?

BECKET. Of course, my Lord.

KING (*with a smile, gently caressing* GWENDOLEN). Well, I won't. I don't want to eat too well every day; it lowers a man's morale. Sadder, sadder, my little doe. (*He belches.*) Oh, that venison! Get her to sing that lament they composed for your mother, Becket. It's my favourite song.

BECKET. I don't like anyone to sing that lament, my Lord.

KING. Why not? Are you ashamed of being a Saracen girl's son? That's half your charm, you fool! There must be some reason why you're more civilized than all the rest of us put together! I adore that song.

GWENDOLEN *looks uncertainly at* BECKET. *There is a pause. Then the* KING *says coldly:*

That's an order, little Saxon.

BECKET (*inscrutably, to* GWENDOLEN).   Sing.

> *She strikes a few opening chords, while the* KING *makes himself comfortable beside her, belching contentedly. She begins.*

GWENDOLEN (*singing*).

Handsome Sir Gilbert
Went to the war
One fine morning in May
To deliver the heart
Of Lord Jesus our Saviour,
From the hands of the Saracens.

Woe! Woe! Heavy is my heart
At being without love!
Woe! Woe! Heavy is my heart
All the livelong day!

KING (*singing*).

All the livelong day!
Go on!

GWENDOLEN.

As the battle raged
He swung his mighty sword
And many a Moor fell dead
But his trusty charger
Stumbled in the fray
And Sir Gilbert fell.

Woe! Woe! Heavy is my heart!
At being without love!
Woe! Woe! Heavy is my heart
All the livelong day.

Wounded in the head
Away Gilbert was led
To the Algiers market
Chained hand and foot
And sold there as a slave.

KING (*singing out of tune*).
All the livelong day!

GWENDOLEN.
A Saracen's daughter
Lovely as the night
Lost her heart to him
Swore to love him always
Vowed to be his wife.

Woe! Woe! Heavy is my heart!
At being without love!
Woe! Woe! Heavy is my heart
All the livelong day —

KING (*interrupting*). It brings tears to my eyes, you know, that story. I look a brute but I'm soft as swansdown really. One can't change one's nature. I can't imagine why you don't like people to sing that song. It's wonderful to be a love child. When I look at my august parents' faces, I shudder to think what must have gone on. It's marvellous to think of your mother helping your father to escape and then coming to join him in London with you inside her. Sing us the end, girl. I adore the end.

GWENDOLEN (*softly*).
Then he asked the holy Father
For a priest to baptise her
And he took her as his wife

To cherish with his life
Give her his soul
To love and keep alway.

Gay! Gay! Easy is my heart
At being full of love
Gay! Gay! Easy is my heart
To be loved alway.

KING (*dreamily*).   Did he really love her all his life? Isn't
it altered a bit in the song?

BECKET.   No, my prince.

KING (*getting up, quite saddened*).   Funny, it's the happy
ending that makes me feel sad. . . . Tell me, do you
believe in love, Thomas?

BECKET (*coldly*).   For my father's love for my mother,
Sire, yes.

> *The* KING *has moved over to the* BARONS, *who are now
> snoring on their stools. He gives them a kick as he
> passes.*

KING.   They've fallen asleep, the hogs. That's their way of
showing their finer feelings. You know, my little Saxon,
sometimes I have the impression that you and I are the
only sensitive men in England. We eat with forks and we
have infinitely distinguished sentiments, you and I.
You've made a different man of me in a way. . . .
What you ought to find me now, if you loved me, is a
girl to give me a little polish. I've had enough of whores.
(*He has come back to* GWENDOLEN. *He caresses her a
little and then says suddenly.*) Favour for favour – do you
remember?

> *A pause.*

BECKET (*pale*).   I am your servant, my prince, and all I
have is yours. But you were also gracious enough to say
I was your friend.

KING.   That's what I mean! As one friend to another it's
the thing to do! (*A short pause. He smiles maliciously, and
goes on caressing* GWENDOLEN, *who cowers, terrified.*)
You care about her, then? Can you care for something?
Go on, tell me, tell me if you care about her? (BECKET
says nothing. The KING *smiles.*) You can't tell a lie. I
know you. Not because you're afraid of lies – I think you
must be the only man I know who isn't afraid of anything
– not even heaven – but because it's distasteful to you.
You consider it inelegant. What looks like morality in
you is nothing more than aesthetics. Is that true or isn't it?

BECKET (*meeting his eye, says softly*).   It's true, my Lord.

KING.   I'm not cheating if I ask for her, am I? I said
'favour for favour' and I asked you for your word of
honour.

BECKET (*icily*).   And I gave it to you.

A pause. They stand quite still. The KING *looks at*
BECKET *with a wicked smile.* BECKET *does not look
at him. Then the* KING *moves briskly away.*

KING.   Right. I'm off to bed. I feel like an early night tonight. Delightful evening, Becket. You're the only man in
England who knows how to give your friends a royal
welcome. (*He kicks the slumbering* BARONS.) Call my
guards and help me wake these porkers.

The BARONS *wake with sighs and belches as the* KING
pushes them about, shouting:

Come on, Barons, home! I know you're connoisseurs of
good music, but we can't listen to music all night long.
Happy evenings end in bed, eh, Becket?

35

BECKET (*stiffly*). May I ask your Highness for a brief moment's grace?

KING. Granted! Granted! I'm not a savage. I'll wait for you both in my litter. You can say good night to me downstairs.

He goes out, followed by the BARONS. BECKET *stands motionless for a while under* GWENDOLEN'S *steady gaze. Then he says quietly:*

BECKET. You will have to go with him, Gwendolen.

GWENDOLEN (*composedly*). Did my Lord promise me to him?

BECKET. I gave him my word as a gentleman that I would give him anything he asked for. I never thought it would be for you.

GWENDOLEN. If he sends me away tomorrow, will my Lord take me back?

BECKET. No.

GWENDOLEN. Shall I tell the girls to put my dresses in the coffer?

BECKET. He'll send over for it tomorrow. Go down. One doesn't keep the King waiting. Tell him I wish him a respectful good night.

GWENDOLEN (*laying her viol on the bed*). I shall leave my Lord my viol. He can almost play it now. (*She asks, quite naturally.*) My Lord cares for nothing in the whole world, does he?

BECKET. No.

GWENDOLEN (*moves to him and says gently*). You belong to a conquered race too. But through tasting too much of the honey of life, you've forgotten that even those who have been robbed of everything, have one thing left to call their own.

BECKET (*inscrutably*). Yes, I daresay I had forgotten.

36

There is a gap in me where honour ought to be. Go now.

> GWENDOLEN *goes out.* BECKET *stands quite still. Then he goes to the bed, picks up the viol, looks at it, and throws it abruptly away. He pulls off the fur coverlet and starts to unbutton his doublet.*
>
> A GUARD *comes in, dragging the* SAXON GIRL *from the forest, whom he throws down in the middle of the room. The* KING *appears.*

KING (*hilariously*). Thomas, my son! You'd forgotten her! You see how careless you are! Luckily I think of everything. It seems they had to bully the father and the brother a tiny bit to get her, but anyway, here she is. You see? – I really am a friend to you, and you're wrong not to love me. You told me you fancied her. I hadn't forgotten that, you see. Sleep well, son!

> *He goes out, followed by the* GUARD. *The* GIRL, *still dazed, looks at* BECKET *who has not moved. She recognizes him, gets to her feet and smiles at him. A long pause, then she asks with a kind of sly coquetry.*

GIRL. Shall I undress, my Lord?
BECKET (*who has not moved*). Of course.

> *The* GIRL *starts to undress.* BECKET *looks at her, coldly, absentmindedly whistling a few bars of his little march. Suddenly he stops, goes to the* GIRL, *who stands there dazed and half naked and seizes her by the shoulders.*

I hope you're full of noble feelings and that all this strikes you as pretty shabby?

> A SERVANT *runs in wildly and halts in the doorway speechless. Before he can speak, the* KING *comes stumbling in.*

KING (*soberly*). I had no pleasure with her, Thomas. She let me lay her down in the litter, limp as a corpse, and then suddenly she pulled out a little knife from somewhere. There was blood everywhere. . . . I feel quite sick. (BECKET *has let go the* GIRL. *The* KING *adds, haggard.*) She could easily have killed me instead! (*A pause. He says abruptly.*) Send that girl away. I'm sleeping in your room tonight. I'm frightened.

> BECKET *motions to the servant, who takes away the half naked* GIRL. *The* KING *has thrown himself, fully dressed, on to the bed with an animal-like sigh.*

Take half the bed.

BECKET. I'll sleep on the floor, my prince.

KING. No. Lie down beside me. I don't want to be alone tonight. (*He looks at him and murmurs.*) You loathe me; I shan't even be able to trust you now. . . .

BECKET. You gave me your seal to keep, my prince. And the three lions of England which are engraved on it keep watch over me too.

> *He snuffs out the candles, all save one. It is almost dark.*

KING (*his voice already thick with sleep*). I shall never know what you're thinking. . . .

> BECKET *has thrown a fur coverlet over the* KING. *He lies down beside him and says quietly:*

BECKET. It will be dawn soon, my prince. You must sleep. Tomorrow we are crossing to the Continent. In a week we will face the King of France's army and there will be simple answers to everything at last.

> *He has lain down beside the* KING. *A pause, during which the* KING'S *snoring gradually increases. Suddenly the* KING *moans and tosses in his sleep.*

KING (*crying out*). They're after me! They're after me! They're armed to the teeth! Stop them! Stop them!

BECKET sits up on one elbow. He touches the KING, *who wakes up with a great animal cry.*

BECKET. My prince ... my prince ... sleep in peace. I'm here.

KING. Oh ... Thomas, it's you.... They were after me.

He turns over and goes back to sleep with a sigh. Gradually he begins to snore again, softly. BECKET *is still on one elbow. Almost tenderly, he draws the coverlet over the* KING.

BECKET. My prince.... If you were my true prince, if you were one of my race, how simple everything would be. How tenderly I would love you, my prince, in an ordered world. Each of us bound in fealty to the other, head, heart and limb, with no further questions to ask of oneself, ever.

A pause. The KING'S *snores grow louder.* BECKET *sighs and says with a little smile.*

But I cheated my way, a twofold bastard, into the ranks, and found a place among the conquerors. You can sleep peacefully, though, my prince. So long as Becket is obliged to improvise his honour, he will serve you. And if one day, he meets it face to face.... (*A short pause.*) But where is Becket's honour?

He lies down with a sigh, beside the KING. *The* KING'S *snores grow louder still. The candle splutters. The lights grow even dimmer....*

CURTAIN

ACT TWO

The curtain rises on the same set of arching pillars, which now represents a forest in France. The KING'S *tent, not yet open for the day, is set up among the trees. A* SENTRY *stands some way off.*

It is dawn. Crouched around a camp fire, the four BARONS *are having their morning meal, in silence. After a while, one of them says:*

FIRST BARON.   This Becket then, who is he?

A pause. All four are fairly slow in their reactions.

SECOND BARON (*surprised at the question*).   The Chancellor of England.

FIRST BARON.   I know that! But who is he, exactly?

SECOND BARON.   The Chancellor of England, I tell you! The Chancellor of England is the Chancellor of England! I don't see what else there is to inquire into on that score.

FIRST BARON.   You don't understand. Look, supposing the Chancellor of England were some other man. Me, for instance. . . .

SECOND BARON.   That's plain idiotic.

FIRST BARON.   I said, supposing. Now, I would be Chancellor of England but I wouldn't be the same Chancellor of England as Becket is. You can follow that, can you?

SECOND BARON (*guardedly*).   Yes. . . .

FIRST BARON.   So, I *can* ask myself the question.

SECOND BARON.   What question?

FIRST BARON.   Who is this man Becket?

40

SECOND BARON. What do you mean, who is this man Becket? He's the Chancellor of England.

FIRST BARON. Yes. But what I'm asking myself is who is he, as a man?

SECOND BARON (*looks at him and says sorrowfully*). Have you got a pain?

FIRST BARON. No, why?

SECOND BARON. A Baron who asks himself questions is a sick Baron. Your sword – what's that?

FIRST BARON. My sword?

SECOND BARON. Yes.

FIRST BARON (*putting his hand to the hilt*). It's my sword! And anyone who thinks different —

SECOND BARON. Right. Answered like a nobleman. We peers aren't here to ask questions. We're here to give answers.

FIRST BARON. Right then. Answer me.

SECOND BARON. Not to questions! To orders. You aren't asked to think in the army. When you're face to face with a French man at arms, do you ask yourself questions?

FIRST BARON. No.

SECOND BARON. Does he?

FIRST BARON. No.

SECOND BARON. You just fall to and fight. If you started asking each other questions like a pair of women, you might as well bring chairs on to the battlefield. If there are any questions to be asked you can be sure they've been asked already, higher up, by cleverer heads than yours.

FIRST BARON (*vexed*). I meant I didn't like him, that's all.

SECOND BARON. Why couldn't you say so, then? That, we'd have understood. You're entitled not to like him. I don't like him either, come to that. To begin with, he's a Saxon.

FIRST BARON. To begin with!

THIRD BARON. One thing you can't say, though. You can't say he isn't a fighter. Yesterday, when the King was in the thick of it, after his squire was killed, he cut his way right through the French, and he seized the King's banner and drew the enemy off and on to himself.

FIRST BARON. All right! He's a good fighter!

THIRD BARON (*to* SECOND BARON). Isn't he a good fighter?

SECOND BARON (*stubbornly*). Yes. But he's a Saxon.

FIRST BARON (*to the* FOURTH BARON, *who has so far said nothing*). How about you, Regnault? What do you think of him?

FOURTH BARON (*placidly*, *swallowing his mouthful of food*). I'm waiting.

FIRST BARON. Waiting for what?

FOURTH BARON. Till he shows himself. Some sorts of game are like that: you follow them all day through the forest, by sounds, or tracks, or smell. But it wouldn't do any good to charge ahead with drawn lance; you'd just spoil everything because you don't know for sure what sort of animal it is you're dealing with. You have to wait.

FIRST BARON. What for?

FOURTH BARON. For whatever beast it is to show itself. And if you're patient it always does in the end. Animals know more than men do, nearly always, but a man has something in him that an animal hasn't got; he knows how to wait. With this man Becket – I'll wait.

FIRST BARON. For what?

FOURTH BARON. For him to show himself. For him to break cover. (*He goes on eating.*) The day he does, we'll know who he is.

42

BECKET'S *little whistled march is heard offstage.* BECKET *comes in, armed.*

BECKET. Good morning to you, gentlemen.

The four BARONS *rise politely, and salute.*

Is the King still asleep?

FIRST BARON (*stiffly*). He hasn't called yet.

BECKET. Has the camp marshal presented his list of losses?

FIRST BARON. No.

BECKET. Why not?

SECOND BARON (*surlily*). He was part of the losses.

BECKET. Oh?

FIRST BARON. I was near by when it happened. A lance knocked him off his horse. Once on the ground, the foot soldiers dealt with him.

BECKET. Poor Beaumont. He was so proud of his new armour.

SECOND BARON. There must have been a chink in it, then. They bled him white. On the ground. French swine!

BECKET (*with a slight shrug*). That's war.

FIRST BARON. War is a sport like any other. There are rules. In the old days, they took you for ransom. A Knight for a Knight. That was proper fighting!

BECKET (*smiling*). Since one has taken to sending the foot-soldiery against the horses with no personal protection save a cutlass, they're a little inclined to seek out the chink in the armour of any Knight unwise enough to fall off his horse. It's repulsive, but I can understand them.

FIRST BARON. If we start understanding the common soldiery war will be butchery, plain and simple.

BECKET. The world is certainly tending towards butchery, Baron. The lesson of this battle, which has cost us far too

43

much, is that we will have to form platoons of cut-throats too, that's all.

FIRST BARON. And a soldier's honour, my Lord Chancellor, what of that?

BECKET (*drily*). A soldier's honour, Baron, is to win victories. Let us not be hypocritical. The Norman nobility lost no time in teaching those they conquered that little point. I'll wake the King. Our entry into the city is timed for eight o'clock and the 'Te Deum' in the cathedral for a quarter past nine. It would be bad policy to keep the French Bishop waiting. We want these people to collaborate with a good grace.

FIRST BARON (*grunting*). In my day, we slaughtered the lot and marched in afterwards.

BECKET. Yes, into a dead city! I want to give the King living cities to increase his wealth. From eight o'clock this morning, I am the French people's dearest friend.

FIRST BARON. What about England's honour, then?

BECKET (*quietly*). England's honour, Baron, in the final reckoning, has always been to succeed.

He goes into the KING'S *tent, smiling. The four* BARONS *look at each other, hostile.*

FIRST BARON (*muttering*). What a mentality!

FOURTH BARON (*sententiously*). We must wait for him. One day, he'll break cover.

The four BARONS *move away.* BECKET *lifts the tent flap and hooks it back. The* KING *is revealed, in bed with a girl.*

KING (*yawning*). Good morning, son. Did you sleep well?

BECKET. A little memento from the French on my left shoulder kept me awake, Sire. I took the opportunity to do some thinking.

KING (*worried*). You think too much. You'll suffer for it,

44

you know! It's because people think that there are problems. One day, if you go on like this, you'll think yourself into a dilemma, your big head will present you with a solution and you'll jump feet first into a hopeless mess – which you'd have done far better to ignore, like the majority of fools, who know nothing and live to a ripe old age. What do you think of my little French girl? I must say, I adore France.

BECKET (*smiling*).   So do I, Sire, like all Englishmen.

KING.   The climate's warm, the girls are pretty, the wine is good. I intend to spend at least a month here every winter.

BECKET.   The only snag is, it's expensive! Nearly two thousand casualties yesterday.

KING.   Has Beaumont made out his total?

BECKET.   Yes. And he added himself to the list.

KING.   Wounded? (BECKET *does not answer. The* KING *shivers. He says sombrely.*) I don't like learning that people I know have died. I've a feeling it may give Death ideas.

BECKET.   My prince, shall we get down to work? We haven't dealt with yesterday's dispatches.

KING.   Yesterday we were fighting! We can't do everything.

BECKET.   That was a holiday! We'll have to work twice as hard today.

KING.   Does it amuse you – working for the good of my people? Do you mean to say you love all those folk? To begin with they're too numerous. One can't love them, one doesn't know them. Anyway, you're lying, you don't love anything or anybody.

BECKET (*tersely*).   There's one thing I do love, my prince, and that I'm sure of. Doing what I have to do and doing it well.

45

KING (*grinning*).   Always the es-es. . . . What's your word
again? – I've forgotten it.

BECKET.   Aesthetics?

KING.   Aesthetics! Always the aesthetic side, eh?

BECKET.   Yes, my prince.

KING (*slapping the* GIRL'S *rump*).   And isn't that aesthetic
too? Some people go into ecstasies over cathedrals. But
this is a work of art too! Look at that – round as an
apple. . . . (*Quite naturally, as if he were offering him a
sweetmeat.*) Want her?

BECKET (*smiling*).   Business, my Lord!

KING (*pouting like a schoolboy*).   All right. Business. I'm
listening. Sit down.

> BECKET *sits down on the bed, beside the* KING, *with the*
> GIRL *like a fascinated rabbit in between them.*

BECKET.   The news is not good, my prince.

KING (*with a careless wave of the hand*).   News never is.
That's a known fact. Life is one long web of difficulties.
The secret of it – and there is one, brought to perfection
by several generations of worldy wise philosophers – is to
give them no importance whatever. In the end one diffi-
culty swallows up the other and you find yourself ten
years later still alive with no harm done. Things always
work out.

BECKET.   Yes. But badly. My prince, when you play
tennis, do you simply sit back and let things work out?
Do you wait for the ball to hit your racquet and say 'It's
bound to come this way eventually'?

KING.   Ah, now just a minute. You're talking about things
that matter. A game of tennis is important, it amuses me.

BECKET.   And suppose I were to tell you that governing
can be as amusing as a game of tennis? Are we going to
let the others smash the ball into our court, my prince, or

46

shall we try to score a point, both of us, like two good English sportsmen?

KING (*suddenly roused by his sporting instinct*). The point, begod, the point! You're right! On the court, I sweat and strain, I fall over my feet, I half kill myself, I'll cheat if need be, but I never give up the point!

BECKET. Well then, I'll tell you what the score is, so far. Piecing together all the information I have received from London since we've been on the Continent, one thing strikes me, and that is: that there exists in England a power which has grown until it almost rivals yours, my Lord. It is the power of your clergy.

KING. We did get them to pay the tax. That's something!

BECKET. Yes, it's a small sum of money. And they know that princes can always be pacified with a little money. But those men are pastmasters at taking back with one hand what they were forced to give with the other. That's a little conjuring trick they've had centuries of practice in.

KING (*to the* GIRL). Pay attention, my little sparrow. Now's your chance to educate yourself. The gentleman is saying some very profound things! . .

BECKET (*in the same flippant way*). Little French sparrow, suppose you educate us instead. When you're married – if you do marry despite the holes in your virtue – which would you prefer: to be mistress in your own house or to have your village priest laying down the law there?

The KING, *a little peeved, gets up on his knees on the bed and hides the bewildered* GIRL *under an eider-down.*

KING. Talk sense, Becket! Priests are always intriguing, I know that. But I also know that I can crush them any time I like.

47

BECKET. Talk sense, Sire. If you don't do the crushing now, in five years' time there will be two Kings in England, the Archbishop of Canterbury and you. And in ten years' time there will be only one.

KING (*a bit shamefaced*). And it won't be me?

BECKET (*coldly*). I rather fear not.

KING (*with a sudden shout*). Oh, yes, it will! We Plantagenets hold on to our own! To horse Becket, to horse! For England's glory! War on the faithful! That will make a change for us!

The eiderdown starts to toss. The GIRL *emerges, dishevelled, and red in the face.*

GIRL (*pleadingly*). My Lord! I can't breathe!

The KING *looks at her in surprise. He had clearly forgotten her. He bursts out laughing.*

KING. What are you doing there? Spying for the clergy? Be off. Put your clothes on and go home. Give her a gold piece, Thomas.

The GIRL *picks up her rags and holds them up in front of her.*

GIRL. Am I to come back to the camp tonight, my Lord?

KING (*exasperated*). Yes. No. I don't know! We're concerned with the Archbishop now, not you! Be off.

The GIRL *disappears into the back portion of the tent. The* KING *cries:*

To horse, Thomas! For England's greatness! With my big fist and your big brain we'll do some good work, you and I! (*With sudden concern.*) Wait a second. You can never be sure of finding another one as good in bed. (*He goes to the rear of the tent and cries.*) Come back tonight, my angel! I adore you! You have the prettiest eyes in the world! (*He comes downstage and says confidentially to* BECKET.) You always have to tell them that, even when you pay for it, if you want real pleasure with them. That's high politics, too! (*Suddenly anxious, as his childish fear of the clergy returns.*) What will God say to it all, though? After all, they're *His* bishops!

BECKET (*with an airy gesture*).   We aren't children. You know one can always come to some arrangement with God, on this earth. Make haste and dress, my prince. We're going to be late.

KING (*hurrying out*).   I'll be ready in a second. Do I have to shave?

BECKET (*smiling*).   It might be as well, after two days' fighting.

KING.   What a fuss for a lot of conquered Frenchmen! I wonder sometimes if you aren't a bit too finicky, Thomas.

He goes out. BECKET *closes the tent just as two* SOLDIERS *bring in a* LITTLE MONK, *with his hands tied.*

BECKET.   What is it?

SOLDIER.   We've just arrested this young monk, my Lord. He was loitering round the camp. He had a knife under his robe. We're taking him to the Provost.

BECKET.   Have you got the knife?

The SOLDIER *hands it to him.* BECKET *looks at it, then at the* LITTLE MONK.

What use do you have for this in your monastery?

LITTLE MONK.   I cut my bread with it!

BECKET (*amused*).   Well, well. (*To the* SOLDIERS.) Leave him to me. I'll question him.

SOLDIER.   He's turbulent, my Lord. He struggled like a

very demon. It took four of us to get his knife away and tie him up. He wounded the sergeant. We'd have finished him there and then, only the sergeant said there might be some information to be got out of him. That's why we're taking him to the Provost. (*He adds.*) That's just to tell you he's a spiteful devil.

BECKET (*who has not taken his eyes off the* LITTLE MONK). Very well. Stand off.

> *The* SOLDIERS *move out of earshot.* BECKET *goes on looking at the* LITTLE MONK, *and playing with the knife.*

What are you doing in France? You're a Saxon.

LITTLE MONK (*crying out despite himself*). How do you know?

BECKET. I can tell by your accent. I speak Saxon very well, as well as you speak French. Yes, you might almost pass for a Frenchman – to unpractised ears. But I'd be careful. In your predicament, you'd do as well to be taken for a Frenchman as a Saxon. It's less unpopular.

> *A pause.*

LITTLE MONK (*abruptly*). I'm prepared to die.

BECKET (*smiling*). After the deed. But before, you'll agree, it's stupid. (*He looks at the knife which he is still holding between two fingers.*) Where are you from?

LITTLE MONK (*venomously*). Hastings!

BECKET. Hastings. And who was this kitchen implement intended for? (*No answer.*) You couldn't hope to kill more than one man with a weapon of this sort. You didn't make the journey for the sake of an ordinary Norman soldier, I imagine.

> *The* LITTLE MONK *does not answer.*

50

(*Tersely.*) Listen to me, my little man. They're going to put you to the torture. Have you ever seen that? I'm obliged to attend professionally from time to time. You think you'll have the necessary strength of spirit, but they're terribly ingenious and they have a knowledge of anatomy that our imbecilic doctors would do well to emulate. One always talks. Believe me, I know. If I can vouch that you've made a full confession, it will go quicker for you. That's worth considering. (*The* MONK *does not answer.*) Besides, there's an amusing detail to this affair. You are directly under my jurisdiction. The King gave me the deeds and livings of all the abbeys in Hastings when he made me Chancellor.

LITTLE MONK (*stepping back*). Are you Becket?

BECKET. Yes. (*He looks at the knife with faint distaste.*) You didn't only use it to cut your bread. Your knife stinks of onion, like any proper little Saxon's knife. They're good, aren't they, the Hastings onions? (*He looks at the knife again with a strange smile.*) You still haven't told me who it was for. (*The* LITTLE MONK *says nothing.*) If you meant it for the King, there was no sense in that, my lad. He has three sons. Kings spring up again like weeds! Did you imagine you could liberate your race single-handed?

LITTLE MONK. No. (*He adds dully.*) Not my race. Myself.

BECKET. Liberate yourself from what?

LITTLE MONK. My shame.

BECKET (*with sudden gravity*). How old are you?

LITTLE MONK. Sixteen.

BECKET (*quietly*). The Normans have occupied the island for a hundred years. Shame is an old vintage. Your father and your grandfather drank it to the dregs. The cup is empty now.

LITTLE MONK (*shaking his head*). No.

51

A shadow seems to cross BECKET'S *eyes. He goes on, quietly.*

BECKET. So, one fine morning, you woke in your cell to the bell of the first offices, while it was still dark. And it was the bells that told you, a boy of sixteen, to take the whole burden of shame on to yourself?

LITTLE MONK (*with the cry of a cornered animal*). Who told you that?

BECKET (*softly*). I told you I was a polyglot. (*Indifferently.*) I'm a Saxon too, did you know that?

LITTLE MONK (*stonily*). Yes.

BECKET (*smiling*). Go on. Spit. You're dying to.

The LITTLE MONK *looks at him, a little dazed, and then spits.*

(*Smiling.*) That felt good, didn't it? (*Tersely.*) The King is waiting. And this conversation could go on indefinitely. But I want to keep you alive, so we can continue it one of these days. (*He adds lightly.*) It's pure selfishness, you know. Your life hasn't any sort of importance for me, obviously, but it's very rare for Fate to bring one face to face with one's own ghost, when young. (*Calling.*) Soldier!

The SOLDIER *comes back and springs clanking to attention.*

Fetch me the Provost. Run!

The SOLDIER *runs out.* BECKET *comes back to the silent* LITTLE MONK.

Delightful day, isn't it? This early morning sun, hot already under this light veil of mist. . . . A beautiful place, France. But I'm like you, I prefer the solid mists of the

52

Sussex downs. Sunshine is luxury. And we belong to a race which used to despise luxury, you and I.

The PROVOST MARSHAL *of the camp comes in, followed by the* SOLDIER. *He is an important personage, but* BECKET *is inaccessible, even for a* PROVOST MARSHAL, *and the man's behaviour shows it.*

Sir Provost, your men have arrested this monk who was loitering round the camp. He is a lay brother from the convent of Hastings and he is directly under my jurisdiction. You will make arrangements to have him sent back to England and taken to the convent, where his Abbot will keep him under supervision until my return. There is no specific charge against him, for the moment. I want him treated without brutality, but very closely watched. I hold you personally responsible for him.

PROVOST. Very good, my Lord.

He motions to the SOLDIERS. *They surround the* LITTLE MONK *and take him away without a further glance from* BECKET. *Left alone,* BECKET *looks at the knife, smiles, wrinkles his nose and murmurs, with faint distaste.*

BECKET. It's touching, but it stinks, all the same. (*He flings the knife away*, and, *whistling his little march, goes towards the tent. He goes in, calling out lightheartedly.*) Well, my Prince, have you put on your Sunday best? It's time to go. We mustn't keep the Bishop waiting!

A sudden joyful peal of bells. The tent disappears as soon as BECKET *has gone in. The set changes. A backcloth representing a street comes down from the flies. The permanent pillars are there, but the* SOLDIERS *lining the route have decorated them with standards. The* KING *and* BECKET *advance into the city, on horse-back, preceded by two* TRUMPETERS; *the* KING *slightly ahead of* BECKET *and followed by the four* BARONS. *Acclamations from the crowd. Bells, trumpets throughout the scene.*

KING (*beaming as he waves*).   Listen to that! They adore us, these French!

BECKET.   It cost me quite a bit. I had money distributed among the populace this morning. The prosperous classes are at home, sulking, of course.

KING.   Patriots?

BECKET.   No. But they would have cost too much. There are also a certain number of your Highness's soldiers among the crowd, in disguise, to encourage any lukewarm elements.

KING.   Why do you always make a game of destroying my illusions? I thought they loved me for myself! You're an amoral man, Becket. (*Anxiously.*) Does one say amoral or immoral?

BECKET (*smiling*).   It depends what one means.

KING.   She's pretty, look – the girl on the balcony to the right there. Suppose we stopped a minute. . . .

BECKET.   Impossible. The Bishop is waiting in the cathedral.

KING.   It would be a lot more fun than going to see a bishop!

BECKET.   My Lord, do you remember what you have to say to him?

KING (*waving to the crowd*).   Yes, yes, yes! As if it mattered what I say to a French bishop, whose city I've just taken by force!

BECKET.   It matters a great deal. For our future policy.

KING.   Am I the strongest or am I not?

BECKET.   You are, today. But one must never drive one's enemy to despair. It makes him strong. Gentleness is better politics. It saps virility. A good occupational force must not crush, it must corrupt.

KING (*waving graciously*).   What about my pleasure, then? Where does that enter into your scheme of things? Suppose I charged into this heap of frog-eaters now instead of acting the goat at their 'Te Deum'? I can indulge in a bit of pleasure, can't I? I'm the conqueror.

BECKET.   That would be a fault. Worse, a failing. One can permit oneself anything, Sire, but one must never indulge.

KING.   Yes, Papa, right, Papa. What a bore you are today. Look at that little redhead there, standing on the fountain! Give orders for the procession to follow the same route back.

He rides on, turning his horse to watch the GIRL *out of sight. They have gone by, the four* BARONS *bringing up the rear. Organ music. The standards disappear, together with the* SOLDIERS. *We are in the cathedral. The stage is empty.*

The organ is heard. Swelling chords. The organist is practising in the empty cathedral. Then a sort of partition is pushed on, which represents the sacristy.

The KING, *attired for the ceremony, the* BARONS, *an unknown* PRIEST *and a* CHOIRBOY *come in. They seem to be waiting for something. The* KING *sits impatiently on a stool.*

KING.   Where's Becket? And what are we waiting for?

FIRST BARON.   He just said to wait, my Lord. It seems there's something not quite in order.

KING (*pacing about ill-humouredly*).   What a lot of fuss for a French bishop! What do I look like, I ask you, hanging about in this sacristy like a village bridegroom!

FOURTH BARON. I quite agree, my Lord! I can't think why we don't march straight in. After all, it's your cathedral now. (*Eagerly*.) What do you say, my Lord? Shall we just draw our swords and charge?

KING (*going meekly back to his stool with a worried frown*). No. Becket wouldn't like it. And he's better than we are at knowing the right thing to do. If he told us to wait, there must be a good reason.

BECKET *hurries in.*

Well, Becket, what's happening? We're freezing to death in here! What do the French think they're at, keeping us mouldering in this sacristy?

BECKET. The order came from me, Sire. A security measure, My police are certain that a French rising was to break out during the ceremony.

The KING *has risen. The* SECOND BARON *has drawn his sword. The other three follow suit.*

SECOND BARON. God's blood!

BECKET. Put up your swords. The King is safe in here. I have put guards on all the doors.

SECOND BARON. Have we your permission to go in and deal with it, my Lord? We'll make short work of it!

THIRD BARON. Just say the word, Sire! Shall we go?

BECKET (*curtly*). I forbid you. There aren't enough of us. I am bringing fresh troops into the city and having the cathedral evacuated. Until that is done, the King's person is in your keeping, gentlemen. But sheath your swords. No provocation, please. We are at the mercy of a chance incident and I still have no more than the fifty escort men at arms in the city.

KING (*tugging at* BECKET'S *sleeve*).   Becket! Is that priest French?

BECKET.   Yes. But he is part of the Bishop's immediate entourage. And the Bishop is our man.

KING.   You know how reliable English bishops are! So I leave you to guess how far we can trust a French one! That man has a funny look in his eyes.

BECKET.   Who, the Bishop?

KING,   No, That priest.

BECKET (*glances at the* PRIEST *and laughs*).   Of course, my prince, he squints! I assure you that's the only disturbing thing about him! It would be tactless to ask him to leave. Besides, even if he had a dagger, you have your coat of mail and four of your barons. I must go and supervise the evacuation of the nave.

He starts to go. The KING *runs after him.*

KING.   Becket! (BECKET *stops.*) The choirboy?

BECKET (*laughing*).   He's only so high!

KING.   He may be a dwarf. You never know with the French. (*Drawing* BECKET *aside.*) Becket, we talked a little flippantly this morning. Are you sure God isn't taking his revenge?

BECKET (*smiling*).   Of course not. I'm afraid it's simply my police force taking fright or being a little over-zealous. Policemen have a slight tendency to see assassins everywhere. They only do it to make themselves important. Bah, what does it matter? We'll hear the 'Te Deum' in a deserted church, that's all.

KING (*bitterly*).   And there was I thinking those folk adored me. Perhaps you didn't give them enough money.

BECKET.   One can only buy those who are for sale, my prince. And those are just the ones who aren't dangerous.

With the others, it's wolf against wolf. I'll come back straight away and set your mind at rest.

He goes out. The KING *darts anxious looks on the* PRIEST *as he paces up and down muttering his prayers.*

KING. Baron!

The FOURTH BARON *is nearest the* KING. *He steps forward.*

FOURTH BARON (*bellowing as usual*). My Lord?
KING. Shush! Keep an eye on that man, all four of you, and at the slightest move, leap on him.

There follows a little comic dumb show by the KING *and the* PRIEST, *who is beginning to feel uneasy too. A sudden violent knocking on the sacristy door. The* KING *starts.*

Who is it?

A SOLDIER *comes in.*

SOLDIER. A messenger from London, my Lord. They sent him on here from the camp. The message is urgent.
KING (*worried*). I don't like it. Regnault, you go and see.

The FOURTH BARON *goes out and comes back again, reassured.*

FOURTH BARON. It's William of Corbeil, my Lord. He has urgent letters.
KING. You're sure it *is* him? It wouldn't be a Frenchman in disguise? That's an old trick.
FOURTH BARON (*roaring with laughter*). I know him, Sire! I've drained more tankards with him than there are whiskers on his face. And the old goat has plenty!

The KING *makes a sign. The* FOURTH BARON *admits the* MESSENGER, *who drops on one knee and presents his letters to the* KING.

KING. Thank you. Get up. That's a fine beard you have, William of Corbeil. Is it well stuck on?

MESSENGER (*rising, bewildered*). My beard, Sire?

The FOURTH BARON *guffaws and slaps him on the back.*

FOURTH BARON. You old porcupine, you!

The KING *has glanced through the letters.*

KING. Good news, gentlemen! We have one enemy less.

BECKET comes in. The KING *cries joyfully:*

Becket!

BECKET. Everything is going according to plan, my prince. The troops are on their way. We've only to wait here quietly, until they arrive.

KING (*cheerfully*). You're right, Becket, everything is going according to plan. God isn't angry with us. He has just recalled the Archbishop.

BECKET (*in a murmur*). That little old man.... How could that feeble body contain so much strength?

KING. Now, now, now! Don't squander your sorrow, my son. I personally consider this an excellent piece of news!

BECKET. He was the first Norman who took an interest in me. He was a true father to me. God rest his soul.

KING. He will! After all the fellow did for Him, he's gone to heaven, don't worry. Where he'll be infinitely more use to God than he was to us. So it's definitely for the best. (*He pulls* BECKET *to him.*) Becket! My little Becket,

59

I think the ball's in our court now! This is the time to score a point. (*He seizes his arm, tense and quite transformed.*) An extraordinary idea is just creeping into my mind, Becket. A master stroke! I can't think what's got into me this morning, but I suddenly feel extremely intelligent. It probably comes of making love with a French girl last night. I am subtle, Becket, I am profound! So profound it's making my head spin. Are you sure it isn't dangerous to think too hard? Thomas, my little Thomas! Are you listening to me?

BECKET (*smiling at his excitement*). Yes, my prince.

KING (*as excited as a little boy*). Are you listening carefully? Listen Thomas! You told me once that the best ideas are the stupidest ones, but the clever thing is to think of them! Listen Thomas! Tradition prevents me from touching the privileges of the primacy. You follow me so far?

BECKET. Yes, my prince. . . .

KING. But what if the Primate is my man? If the Archbishop of Canterbury is for the King, how can his power possibly incommodate me?

BECKET. That's an ingenious idea, my prince, but you forget that his election is a free one.

KING. No! You're forgetting the Royal Hand! Do you know what that is? When the candidate is displeasing to the Throne the King sends his Justicer to the Conclave of Bishops and it's the King who has the final say. That's an old custom too, and for once, it's in my favour! It's fully a hundred years since the Conclave of Bishops has voted contrary to the wishes of the King!

BECKET. I don't doubt it, my Lord. But we all know your bishops. Which one of them could you rely on? Once the Primate's mitre is on their heads, they grow dizzy with power.

KING. Are you asking me, Becket? I'll tell you. Someone who doesn't know what dizziness means. Someone who isn't even afraid of God. Thomas, my son, I need your help again and this time it's important. I'm sorry to deprive you of French girls and the fun of battle, my son, but pleasure will come later. You are going over to England.

BECKET. I am at your service, my prince.

KING. Can you guess what your mission will be?

A tremor of anguish crosses BECKET'S *face at what is to come.*

BECKET. No, my prince.

KING. You are going to deliver a personal letter from me to every bishop in the land. And do you know what those letters will contain, my Thomas, my little brother? My royal wish to have you elected Primate of England.

BECKET *has gone deathly white. He says with a forced laugh:*

BECKET. You're joking, of course, my Lord. Just look at the edifying man, the saintly man whom you would be trusting with these holy functions! (*He has opened his fine coat to display his even finer doublet.*) Why, my prince, you really fooled me for a second! (*The* KING *bursts out laughing.* BECKET *laughs too, rather too loudly in his relief.*) A fine Archbishop I'd have made! Look at my new shoes! They're the latest fashion in Paris. Attractive, that little upturned toe, don't you think? Quite full of unction and compunction, isn't it, Sire?

KING (*suddenly stops laughing*). Shut up about your shoes, Thomas! I'm in deadly earnest. I shall write those letters before noon. You will help me.

BECKET, *deathly pale, stammers.*

BECKET. But my Lord, I'm not even a priest!

KING (*tersely*). You're a deacon. You can take your final vows tomorrow and be ordained in a month.

BECKET. But have you considered what the Pope will say?

KING (*brutally*). I'll pay the price!

BECKET, *after an anguished pause, murmurs:*

BECKET. My Lord, I see now that you weren't joking. Don't do this.

KING. Why not?

BECKET. It frightens me.

KING (*his face set and hard*). Becket, this is an order!

BECKET *stands as if turned to stone. A pause. He murmurs:*

BECKET (*gravely*). If I become Archbishop, I can no longer be your friend.

A burst of organ music in the cathedral. Enter an OFFICER.

OFFICER. The church is now empty, my Lord. The Bishop and his clergy await your Highness's good pleasure.

KING (*roughly to* BECKET). Did you hear that, Becket? Pull yourself together. You have an odd way of taking good news. Wake up! They say we can go in now.

The procession forms with the PRIEST *and the* CHOIR-BOY *leading.* BECKET *takes his place, almost reluctantly, a pace or so behind the* KING.

BECKET (*in a murmur*). This is madness, my Lord. Don't do it. I could not serve both God and you.

KING (*looking straight ahead, says stonily*). You've never disappointed me, Thomas. And you are the only man I trust. You will leave tonight. Come, let's go in.

He motions to the PRIEST. *The procession moves off and goes into the empty cathedral, as the organ swells.*

A moment's darkness. The organ continues to play. Then a dim light reveals BECKET'S *room. Open chests into which two* SERVANTS *are piling costly clothes.*

SECOND SERVANT (*the younger of the two*). The coat with the sable trimming as well?

FIRST SERVANT. Everything! You heard what he said!

SECOND SERVANT (*grumbling*). Sables! To beggars! Who'll give them alms if they beg with that on their backs! They'll starve to death!

FIRST SERVANT (*cackling*). They'll eat the sables! Can't you understand, you idiot! He's going to sell all this and give them the money!

SECOND SERVANT. But what will he wear himself? He's got nothing left at all!

BECKET *comes in, wearing a plain grey dressing-gown.*

BECKET. Are the chests full? I want them sent over to the Jew before tonight. I want nothing left in this room but the bare walls. Gil, the fur coverlet!

FIRST SERVANT (*regretfully*). My Lord will be cold at night.

BECKET. Do as I say.

Regretfully, the FIRST SERVANT *takes the coverlet and puts it in the chest.*

Has the steward been told about tonight's meal? Supper for forty in the great hall.

FIRST SERVANT. He says he won't have enough gold plate, my Lord. Are we to mix it with the silver dishes?

BECKET. Tell him to lay the table with the wooden

63

platters and earthenware bowls from the kitchens. The plate has been sold. The Jew will send over for it late this afternoon.

FIRST SERVANT (*dazed*). The earthenware bowls and the wooden platters. Yes, my Lord. And the steward says could he have your list of invitations fairly soon, my Lord. He only has three runners and he's afraid there won't be time to —

BECKET. There are no invitations. The great doors will be thrown open and you will go out into the street and tell the poor they are dining with me tonight.

FIRST SERVANT (*appalled*). Very good, my Lord.

He is about to go. BECKET *calls him back.*

BECKET. I want the service to be impeccable. The dishes presented to each guest first, with full ceremony, just as for princes. Go now.

The two SERVANTS *go out.* BECKET, *left alone, casually looks over one or two articles of clothing in the chests. He murmurs:*

I must say it was all very pretty stuff.

He drops the lid and bursts out laughing.

A prick of vanity! The mark of an upstart. A truly saintly man would never have done the whole thing in one day. Nobody will ever believe it's genuine. (*He turns to the jewelled crucifix above the bed and says simply.*) I hope you haven't inspired me with all these holy resolutions in order to make me look ridiculous, Lord? It's all so new to me. I'm setting about it a little clumsily perhaps. (*He looks at the crucifix and with a swift gesture takes it off the wall.*) And you're far too sumptuous too. Precious stones around your bleeding Body. . . . I shall give you to some poor village church.

He lays the crucifix on the chest. He looks around the
room, happy, light-hearted, and murmurs:

It's like leaving for a holiday. Forgive me, Lord, but I
never enjoyed myself so much in my whole life. I don't
believe You are a sad God. The joy I feel in shedding all
my riches must be a part of Your divine intentions.

*He goes behind the curtain into the antechamber where
he can be heard gaily whistling an old English marching song. He comes back a second later, his bare feet
in sandals, and wearing a monk's coarse woollen robe.
He draws the curtain across again and murmurs:*

BECKET.   There. Farewell, Becket. I wish there had been
something I had regretted parting with, so I could offer
it to You. (*He goes to the crucifix and says simply.*) Lord,
are you sure you are not tempting me? It all seems far
too easy.

He drops to his knees and prays.

CURTAIN

65

ACT THREE

A room in the KING'S *palace. The two* QUEENS, *the* QUEEN
MOTHER *and the* YOUNG QUEEN *are on stage, working
at their tapestry. The* KING'S *two* SONS, *one consider-
ably older than the other, are playing in a corner, on the
floor. The* KING *is in another corner, playing at cup-and-
ball. After several unsuccessful attempts to catch the ball
in the cup, he throws down the toy and exclaims irritably:*

KING. Forty beggars! He invited forty beggars to dinner!

QUEEN MOTHER. The dramatic gesture, as usual! I
always said you had misplaced your confidence, my son.

KING (*pacing up and down*). Madam, I am very particular
where I place my confidence. I only ever did it once in my
whole life and I am still convinced I was right. But there's
a great deal we don't understand! Thomas is ten times
more intelligent than all of us put together.

QUEEN MOTHER (*reprovingly*). You are talking about
royalty, my son.

KING (*grunting*). What of it? Intelligence has been shared
out on a different basis.

YOUNG QUEEN. It seems he has sold his gold plate and
all his rich clothes to a Jew. He wears an ordinary home-
spun habit now.

QUEEN MOTHER. I see that as a sign of ostentation, if
nothing worse! One can become a saintly man, certainly,
but not in a single day. I've never liked the man. You were
insane to make him so powerful.

KING (*crying out*).   He is my friend!

QUEEN MOTHER (*acidly*).   More's the pity.

YOUNG QUEEN.   He is your friend in debauchery. It was he who lured you away from your duty towards me. It was he who first took you to the whorehouses!

KING (*furious*).   Rubbish, Madam! I didn't need anybody to lure me away from my duty towards you. I made you three children, very conscientiously. Phew! My duty is done for a while.

YOUNG QUEEN (*stung*).   When that libertine loses the evil influence he has on you, you will come to appreciate the joys of family life again. Pray Heaven he disobeys you!

KING.   The joys of family life are limited, Madam. To be perfectly frank, you bore me. You and your eternal back-biting, over your everlasting tapestry, the pair of you! That's no sustenance for a man! (*He trots about the room, furious, and comes to a halt behind their chairs.*) If at least it had some artistic merit. My ancestress Mathilda, while she was waiting for her husband to finish carving out his kingdom, now *she* embroidered a masterpiece – which they left behind in Bayeux, more's the pity. But that! It's beyond belief, it's so mediocre.

YOUNG QUEEN (*nettled*).   We can only use the gifts we're born with.

KING.   Yes. And yours are meagre. (*He glances out of the window once more to look at the time, and says with a sigh.*) I've been bored to tears for a whole month. Not a soul to talk to. After his nomination, not wanting to seem in too indecent a hurry, I leave him alone to carry out his pastoral tour. Now, back he comes at last; I summon him to the palace and he's late. (*He looks out of the window again and exclaims.*) Ah! Someone at the sentry post! (*He turns away, disappointed.*) No, it's only a monk.

67

He wanders about the room, aimlessly. He goes over to join the children, and watches them playing for a while.

(*Sourly.*) Charming babes. Men in the making. Sly and obtuse already. And to think one is expected to be dewy-eyed over creatures like that, merely because they aren't yet big enough to be hated or despised. Which is the elder of you two?

ELDER BOY (*rising*). I am, Sir.

KING. What's your name again?

ELDER BOY. Henry III.

KING (*sharply*). Not yet, Sir! Number II is in the best of health. (*To the* QUEEN.) You've brought them up well! Do you think of yourself as Regent already? And you wonder that I shun your bedchamber? I don't care to make love with my widow.

An OFFICER *comes in.*

OFFICER. A messenger from the Archbishop, my Lord.

KING (*beside himself with rage*). A messenger! A messenger! I summoned the Archbishop Primate in person! (*He turns to the women, suddenly uneasy, almost touching.*) Perhaps he's ill? That would explain everything.

QUEEN MOTHER (*bitterly*). That's too much to hope for.

KING (*raging*). You'd like to see him dead, wouldn't you, you females – because he loves me? If he hasn't come, it's because he's dying! Send the man in, quickly! O my Thomas. . . .

The OFFICER *goes and admits the* MONK. *The* KING *hurries over to him.*

Who are you? Is Becket ill?

MONK (*falling on one knee*). My Lord, I am William, son of Etienne, secretary to his Grace the Archbishop.

KING. Is your master seriously ill?

MONK. No, my Lord. His Grace is in good health. He has charged me to deliver this letter with his deepest respects – and to give your Highness this. (*He bows lower and hands something to the* KING.)

KING (*stunned*). The seal? Why has he sent me back the seal? (*He unrolls the parchment and reads it in silence. His face hardens. He says curtly, without looking at the* MONK.) You have carried out your mission. Go.

The MONK *rises and turns to go.*

MONK. Is there an answer from your Highness for His Grace the Archbishop?

KING (*harshly*). No!

The MONK *goes out. The* KING *stands still a moment, at a loss, then flings himself on to his throne, glowering. The* WOMEN *exchange a conspiratorial look. The* QUEEN MOTHER *rises and goes to him.*

QUEEN MOTHER (*insidiously*). Well, my son, what does your friend say in his letter?

KING (*bawling*). Get out! Get out, both of you! And take your royal vermin with you! I am alone!

Frightened, the QUEENS *hurry out with the* CHILDREN. *The* KING *stands there a moment, reeling a little, as if stunned by the blow. Then he collapses on to the throne and sobs like a child.*

(*Moaning.*) O my Thomas!

He remains a moment prostrate, then collects himself and sits up. He looks at the seal in his hand and says between clenched teeth:

You've sent me back the three lions of England, like a

little boy who doesn't want to play with me any more. You think you have God's Honour to defend now! I would have gone to war with all England's might behind me, and against England's interests, to defend you, little Saxon. I would have given the honour of the kingdom laughingly ... for you.... Only I loved you and you didn't love me ... that's the difference. (*His face hardens. He adds between clenched teeth.*) Thanks all the same for this last gift as you desert me. I shall learn to be alone.

> *He goes out. The lights dim.* SERVANTS *remove the furniture. When the lights go up again, the permanent set, with the pillars, is empty.*

> *A bare church; a* MAN *half hidden under a dark cloak is waiting behind a pillar. It is the* KING. *Closing chords of organ music. Enter* GILBERT FOLLIOT, BISHOP OF LONDON, *followed by his clergy. He has just said mass. The* KING *goes to him.*

Bishop. . . .

FOLLIOT (*stepping back*).   What do you want, fellow? (*His* ACOLYTES *are about to step between them, when he exclaims.*) The King!

KING.   Yes.

FOLLIOT.   Alone, without an escort, and dressed like a common squire?

KING.   The King nevertheless. Bishop, I would like to make confession.

FOLLIOT (*with a touch of suspicion*).   I am the Bishop of London. The King has his own confessor. That is an important Court appointment and it has its prerogatives.

KING.   The choice of priest for holy confession is open, Bishop, even for a King.

> FOLLIOT *motions to his* CLERGY, *who draw away.*

Anyway, my confession will be short, and I'm not asking for absolution. I have something much worse than a sin on my conscience, Bishop: a mistake. A foolish mistake. (FOLLIOT *says nothing*.) I ordered you to vote for Thomas Becket at the Council of Clarendon. I repent of it.

FOLLIOT (*inscrutably*).   We bowed before the Royal Hand.

KING.   Reluctantly, I know. It took me thirteen weeks of authority and patience to crush the small uncrushable opposition of which you were the head, Bishop. On the day the Council met you looked green. They told me you fell seriously ill afterwards.

FOLLIOT (*impenetrably*).   God cured me.

KING.   Very good of Him. But He is rather inclined to look after His own, to the exclusion of anyone else. He let me fall ill without lifting a finger! And I must cure myself without divine intervention. I have the Archbishop on my stomach. A big hard lump I shall have to vomit back. What does the Norman clergy think of him?

FOLLIOT (*reserved*).   His Grace seems to have the reins of the Church of England well in hand. Those who are in close contact with him even say that he behaves like a holy man.

KING (*with grudging admiration*).   It's a bit sudden, but nothing he does ever surprises me. God knows what the brute is capable of, for good or for evil. Bishop, let us be frank with each other. Is the Church very interested in holy men?

FOLLIOT (*with a ghost of a smile*).   The Church has been wise for so long, your Highness, that she could not have failed to realize that the temptation of saintliness is one of the most insidious and fearsome snares the devil can lay for her priests. The administration of the realm of souls, with the temporal difficulties it carries with it, chiefly demands, as in all administrations, competent administrators. The Roman Catholic Church has its saints, it invokes their benevolent intercession, it prays to them. But it has no need to create others. That is superfluous. And dangerous.

KING. You seem to be a man one can talk to, Bishop. I misjudged you. Friendship blinded me.

FOLLIOT (*still impenetrable*). Friendship is a fine thing.

KING (*suddenly human*). It's a domestic animal, a living, tender thing. It seems to be all eyes, forever gazing at you, warming you. You don't see its teeth. But it's a beast with one curious characteristic. It is only after death that it bites.

FOLLIOT (*prudently*). Is the King's friendship for Thomas Becket dead, your Highness?

KING. Yes, Bishop. It died quite suddenly. A sort of heart failure.

FOLLIOT. A curious phenomenon, your Highness, but quite frequent.

KING (*taking his arm suddenly*). I hate Becket now, Bishop. There is nothing more in common between that man and me than this creature tearing at my guts. I can't bear it any more. I shall have to turn it loose on him. But I am the King; what they conventtionally call my greatness stands in my way. I need somebody.

FOLLIOT (*stiffening*). I do not wish to serve anything but the Church.

KING. Let us talk like grown men, Bishop. We went in hand in hand to conquer, pillage and ransom England. We quarrel, we try to cheat each other of a penny or two, but heaven and earth still have one or two common interests. Do you know what I have just obtained from the Pope? His blessing to go and murder Catholic Ireland, in the name of the Faith. Yes, a sort of crusade to impose Norman barons and clergy on the Irish, with our swords and standards solemnly blessed as if we were off to give the Turks a drubbing. The only condition: a little piece of silver per household per year, for St. Peter's pence, which the native clergy of Ireland is loth to part with and which I have undertaken to make them pay. It's a mere pittance. But at the end of the year it will add up to a pretty sum. Rome knows how to do her accounts.

FOLLIOT (*terror stricken*). There are some things one should never say, your Highness; one should even try not to know about them, so long as one is not directly concerned with them.

KING (*smiling*). We are alone, Bishop, and the Church is empty.

FOLLIOT. The Church is never empty. A little red lamp burns in front of the High Altar.

KING (*impatiently*). Bishop, I like playing games, but only with boys of my own age! Do you take me for one of your sheep, holy pastor? The One whom that little red lamp honours read into your innermost heart and mine a long time ago. Of your cupidity and my hatred, He knows all there is to know.

> FOLLIOT *withdraws into his shell. The* KING *cries irritably:*

If that's the way you feel you must become a monk, Bishop! Wear a hairsuit on your naked back and go and hide yourself in a monastery to pray! The Bishopric of London, for the pure-hearted son of a Thames waterman, is too much, or too little!

> *A pause.*

FOLLIOT (*impassively*). If, as is my duty, I disregard my private feelings, I must admit that His Grace the Archbishop has so far done nothing which has not been in the interests of Mother Church.

KING (*eyeing him, says jovially*).   I can see your game, my little friend. You mean to cost me a lot of money. But I'm rich – thanks to Becket, who has succeeded in making you pay the Absentee Tax. And it seems to me eminently ethical that a part of the Church's gold should find its way, via you, back to the Church. Besides, if we want to keep this on a moral basis, holy Bishop, you can tell yourself that as the greatness of the Church and that of the State are closely linked, in serving me, you will in the long run be working for the consolidation of the Catholic Faith.

FOLLIOT (*contemplating him with curiosity*).   I had always taken your Highness for a great adolescent lout who cared only for his pleasure.

KING.   One can be wrong about people, Bishop. I made the same mistake. (*With a sudden cry.*) O my Thomas. . . .

FOLLIOT (*fiercely*).   You love him, your Highness! You still love him! You love that mitred hog, that impostor, that Saxon bastard, that little guttersnipe!

KING (*seizing him by the throat*).   Yes, I love him! But that's my affair, priest! All I confided to you was my hatred. I'll pay you to rid me of him, but don't ever speak ill of him to me. Or we'll fight it out as man to man!

FOLLIOT.   Highness, you're choking me!

KING (*abruptly releasing him*).   We will meet again to-morrow, my Lord Bishop, and we'll go over the details of our enterprise together. You will be officially summoned to the Palace on some pretext or other – my good works in your London diocese, say – where I am your chief parishioner. But it won't be the poor and needy we'll discuss. My poor can wait. The kingdom they pin their hopes on is eternal.

The KING *goes out.* GILBERT FOLLIOT *remains motion-less. His* CLERGY *join him timidly. He takes his crook and goes out with dignity, but not before one of his* CANONS *has discreetly adjusted his mitre, which was knocked askew in the recent struggle. They have gone out.*

The lighting changes. Curtains between the pillars. The episcopal palace.

Morning. A PRIEST *enters, leading two* MONKS *and the* LITTLE MONK *from the convent of Hastings.*

PRIEST.   His Grace will receive you here.

The two MONKS *are impressed. They push the* LITTLE MONK *about a little.*

FIRST MONK.   Stand up straight. Kiss his Grace's ring and try to answer his questions with humility, or I'll tan your backside for you!

SECOND MONK.   I suppose you thought he'd forgotten all about you? The great never forget anything. And don't you act proud with him or you'll be sorry.

Enter BECKET, *wearing a coarse monk's robe.*

BECKET.   Well, brothers, is it fine over in Hastings?

He gives them his ring to kiss.

FIRST MONK.   Foggy, my Lord.

BECKET (*smiling*).   Then it's fine in Hastings. We always think fondly of our abbey there and we intend to visit it soon, when our new duties grant us a moment's respite. How has this young man been behaving? Has he given our Abbot much trouble?

SECOND MONK.   A proper mule, my Lord. Father Abbot

tried kindness, as you recommended, but he soon had to have recourse to the dungeon and bread and water, and even to the whip. Nothing has any effect. The stubborn little wretch is just the same; all defiance and insults. He has fallen into the sin of pride. Nothing I know of will pull him out of that!

FIRST MONK. Save a good kick in the rump perhaps – if your Grace will pardon the expression. (*To the* LITTLE MONK.) Stand up straight.

BECKET (*to the* LITTLE MONK). Pay attention to your brother. Stand up straight. As a rule the sin of pride stiffens a man's back. Look me in the face. (*The* LITTLE MONK *looks at him.*) Good.

> BECKET *looks at the* LITTLE MONK *for a while, then turns to the* MONKS.

You will be taken to the kitchens where you can refresh yourselves before you leave, brothers. They have orders to treat you well. Don't spurn our hospitality; we relieve you, for today, of your vows of abstinence, and we fondly hope you will do honour to our bill of fare. Greet your father Abbot in Jesus on our behalf.

SECOND MONK (*hesitantly*). And the lad?

BECKET. We will keep him here.

FIRST MONK. Watch out for him, your Grace. He's vicious.

BECKET (*smiling*). We are not afraid.

> *The* MONKS *go out.* BECKET *and the* LITTLE MONK *remain, facing each other.*

Why do you hold yourself so badly?

LITTLE MONK. I don't want to look people in the face any more.

BECKET. I'll teach you. That will be your first lesson.

76

Look at me. (*The* LITTLE MONK *gives him a sidelong glance.*) Better than that. (*The* LITTLE MONK *looks at him.*) Are you still bearing the full weight of England's shame alone? Is it that shame which bends your back like that?

LITTLE MONK. Yes.

BECKET. If I took over half of it, would it weigh less heavy? (*He motions to the* PRIEST.) Show in their Lordships the bishops. You'll soon see that being alone is not a privilege reserved entirely for you.

> *The* BISHOPS *come in.* BECKET *leads the* LITTLE MONK *into a corner.*

You stay here in the corner and hold my tablets. I ask only one thing. Don't leap at their throats; you'd complicate everything. (*He motions to the* BISHOPS, *who remain standing.*)

FOLLIOT. Your Grace, I am afraid this meeting may be a pointless one. You insisted – against our advice – on attacking the King openly. Even before the three excommunications which you asked us to sanction could be made public, the King has hit back. His Grand Justicer Richard de Lacy has just arrived in your ante-chamber and is demanding to see you in the name of the King. He is the bearer of an official order summoning you to appear before his assembled council within twenty-four hours and there to answer the charges made against you.

BECKET. Of what is the King accusing me?

FOLLIOT. Prevarication. Following the examination of accounts by his Privy Council, his Highness demands a considerable sum still outstanding on your administration of the Treasury.

BECKET. When I resigned the Chancellorship I handed over my ledgers to the Grand Justicer, who acquitted me

77

of all subsequent dues and claims. What does the King demand?

OXFORD. Forty thousand marks in fine gold.

BECKET (*smiling*). I don't believe there was ever as much money in all the coffers of all England in all the time I was Chancellor. But a clever clerk can soon change that. ... The King has closed his fist and I am like a fly inside it. (*He smiles and looks at them.*) I have the impression, gentlemen, that you must be feeling something very akin to relief.

YORK. We advised you against open opposition.

BECKET. William of Aynsford, incited by the King, struck down the priest I had appointed to the parish of his Lordship's see, on the pretext that his Highness disapproved of my choice. Am I to look on while my priests are murdered?

FOLLIOT. It is not for you to appoint a priest to a free fief! There is not a Norman, layman or cleric, who will ever concede that. It would mean reviewing the entire legal system of the Conquest. Everything that can be called into question in England except the fact that it was conquered in 1066. England is the land of law and of the most scrupulous respect for the law; but the law begins at that date only, or England as such ceases to exist.

BECKET. Bishop, must I remind you that we are men of God and that we have an honour to defend, which dates from all eternity?

OXFORD (*quietly*). This excommunication was bad policy, your Grace. William of Aynsford is a companion of the King.

BECKET (*smiling*). I know him very well. He's a charming man. I have drained many a tankard with him.

YORK (*yelping*). And his wife is my second cousin!

BECKET. That is a detail I deplore, my Lord Bishop, but

he has killed one of my priests. If I do not defend my priests, who will? Gilbert of Clare has indicted before his court of justice a churchman who was under our exclusive jurisdiction.

YORK. An interesting victim, I must say! He deserved the rope a hundred times over. The man was accused of rape and murder. Wouldn't it have been cleverer to let the wretch hang – and have peace?

BECKET. 'I bring not peace but the sword'. Your Lordship must I'm sure have read that somewhere. I am not interested in what this man is guilty of. If I allow my priests to be tried by a secular tribunal, if I let Robert de Vere abduct our tonsured clerics from our monasteries, as he has just done, on the grounds that the man was one of his serfs who had escaped land bondage, I don't give much for our freedom and our chances of survival in five years time, my Lord. I have excommunicated Gilbert of Clare, Robert de Vere and William of Aynsford. The kingdom of God must be defended like any other kingdom. Do you think that Right has only to show its handsome face for everything to drop into its lap? Without Might, its old enemy, Right counts for nothing.

YORK. What Might? Let us not indulge in empty words. The King is Might and he is the law.

BECKET. He is the written law, but there is another, unwritten law, which always makes kings bend the neck eventually. (*He looks at them for a moment and smiles.*) I was a profligate, gentlemen, perhaps a libertine, in any case, a worldly man. I loved living and I laughed at all these things. But you passed the burden on to me and now I have to carry it. I have rolled up my sleeves and taken it on my back and nothing will ever make me set it down again. I thank your Lordships. The council is adjourned and I have made my decision. I shall stand by these three

79

excommunications. And I shall appear tomorrow before the King's supreme Court of Justice.

The BISHOPS *look at one another in surprise, then bow and go out.* BECKET *turns to the* LITTLE MONK.

Well, does the shame weigh less heavy now?

LITTLE MONK. Yes.

BECKET (*leading him off and laughing*). Then stand up straight!

The curtains close. Distant trumpets. The KING *comes out from behind the curtains and turns to peep through them at something. A pause. Then* GILBERT FOLLIOT *comes hurrying in.*

KING. What's happening? I can't see a thing from up here.

FOLLIOT. Legal procedure is taking its course, your Highness. The third summons has been delivered. He has not appeared. In a moment he will be condemned *in absentia*. Once prevarication is established, our dean the Bishop of Chichester will go to see him and communicate according to the terms of the ancient charter of the Church of England, our corporate repudiation of allegiance, absolving us of obedience to him – and our intention to report him to our Holy Father the Pope. I shall then, as Bishop of London, step forward and publicly accuse Becket of having celebrated, in contempt of the King, a sacrilegious mass at the instigation of the Evil Spirit.

KING (*anxiously*). Isn't that going rather far?

FOLLIOT. Of course. It won't fool anyone, but it always works. The assembly will then go out to vote, in order of precedence, and return a verdict of imprisonment. The sentence is already drawn up.

KING.   Unanimously?

FOLLIOT.   We are all Normans. The rest is your Highness's concern. It will merely be a matter of carrying out the sentence.

KING (*staggering suddenly*).   O my Thomas!

FOLLIOT (*impassively*).   I can still stop the machine, your Highness.

KING (*hesitates a second, then says*).   No. Go.

> FOLLIOT *goes out. The* KING *goes back to his palace, behind the curtain.*

> *The* TWO QUEENS *come into the room, and join the* KING. *All three stand and peer through the curtain. A pause.*

YOUNG QUEEN.   He's doomed, isn't he?

KING (*dully*).   Yes.

YOUNG QUEEN.   At last!

> *The* KING *turns on her, his face twisted with hate.*

KING.   I forbid you to gloat!

YOUNG QUEEN.   At seeing your enemy perish – why not?

KING (*frothing*).   Becket is my enemy, but in the human balance, bastard as he is, and naked as his mother made him, he weighs a hundred more times than you do, Madam, with your crown and all your jewels and your august father the Emperor into the bargain. Becket is attacking me and he has betrayed me. I am forced to fight him and crush him, but at least he gave me, with open hands, everything that is at all good in me. And you have never given me anything but your carping mediocrity, your everlasting obsession with your puny little person and what you thought was due to it. That is why I forbid you to smile as he lies dying!

YOUNG QUEEN. I gave you my youth! I gave you your children!

KING (*shouting*). I don't like my children! And as for your youth – that dusty flower pressed in a hymn book since you were twelve years old, with its watery blood and its insipid scent – you can say farewell to that without a tear. With age, bigotry and malice may perhaps give some spice to your character. Your body was an empty desert, Madam – which duty forced me to wander in alone! But you have never been a wife to me! And Becket was my friend, red-blooded, generous and full of strength. (*He is shaken by a sob.*) O my Thomas!

The QUEEN MOTHER *moves over to him.*

QUEEN MOTHER (*haughtily*). And I, my son, I gave you nothing either, I suppose?

KING (*recovers his composure, glares at her and says dully*). Life. Yes. Thank you. But after that I never saw you save in a passage, dressed for a ball, or in your crown and ermine mantle, ten minutes before official ceremonies, where you were forced to tolerate my presence. I have always been alone, and no one on this earth has ever loved me except Becket!

QUEEN MOTHER (*bitterly*). Well, call him back! Absolve him, since he loves you! Give him supreme power then! But do something!

KING. I am. I'm learning to be alone again, Madam. As usual.

A PAGE *comes in, breathless.*

Well? What's happening? How far have they got?

PAGE. My Liege, Thomas Becket appeared just when everyone had given him up; sick, deathly pale, in full pontifical regalia and carrying his own heavy silver cross. He walked the whole length of the hall without

anyone daring to stop him, and when Robert, Duke of
Leicester, who was to read out his sentence, began the
consecrated words, he stopped him with a gesture and
forbade him, in God's name, to pronounce judgement
against him, his spiritual father. Then he walked back
through the crowd, which parted for him in silence. He
has just left.

KING (*unable to hide his delight*).   Well played, Thomas!
One point to you. (*He checks himself, embarrassed, and
then says.*) And what about my barons?

PAGE.   Their hands flew to their swords with cries of
'Traitor! Perjurer! Arrest him! Miserable wretch! Hear
your sentence!' But not one of them dared move, or
touch the sacred ornaments.

KING (*with a roar*).   The fools! I am surrounded by fools
and the only intelligent man in my kingdom is against
me!

PAGE (*continuing his story*).   Then, on the threshold, he
turned, looked at them coldly as they shouted in their
impotence, and he said that not so long ago he could
have answered their challenge sword in hand. Now he
could no longer do it, but he begged them to remember
that there was a time when he met strength with strength.

KING (*jubilantly*).   He could beat them all! All, I tell you!
On horseback, on foot, with a mace, with a lance, with a
sword! In the lists they fell to him like ninepins!

PAGE.   And his eyes were so cold, and so ironic – even
though all he had in his hand was his episcopal crook,
that one by one they fell silent. Only then did he turn and
go out. They say he has given orders to invite all the
beggars of the city to sup at his house tonight.

KING (*sombrely*).   And what about the Bishop of London,
who was going to reduce him to powder? What about my
busy friend, Gilbert Folliot?

PAGE. He had a horrible fit of rage, trying to incite the crowd, he let out a screech of foul abuse and then fainted. They are bringing him round now.

The KING *suddenly bursts into a shout of irrepressible laughter, and, watched by the two outraged* QUEENS, *collapses into the* PAGE'S *arms, breathless and helpless with mirth.*

KING. It's too funny! It's too funny!

QUEEN MOTHER (*coldly*). You will laugh less heartily tomorrow, my son. If you don't stop him, Becket will reach the coast tonight, ask asylum of the King of France and jeer at you, unpunished, from across the Channel.

She sweeps out with the YOUNG QUEEN. *Suddenly, the* KING *stops laughing and runs out.*

The light changes. The curtains part. We are at the Court of LOUIS, KING OF FRANCE. *He is sitting in the middle of the courtroom, very erect on his throne. He is a burly man with intelligent eyes.*

LOUIS (*to his* BARONS). Gentlemen, we are in France, and a pox on England's King – as the song goes.

FIRST BARON. Your Majesty cannot *not* receive his ambassadors extraordinary!

LOUIS. Ordinary, or extraordinary, I am at home to all ambassadors. It's my job. I shall receive them.

FIRST BARON. They have been waiting in your Majesty's anteroom for over an hour, Sire.

LOUIS. Let them wait. That's *their* job. An ambassador is made for pacing about an antechamber. I know what they are going to ask me.

SECOND BARON. The extradition of a felon is a courtesy due from one crowned head to another.

84

LOUIS.   My dear men, crowned heads can play the little game of courtesy but nations owe each other none. My right to play the courteous gentleman stops where France's interests begin. And France's interests consist in making things as difficult as possible for England – a thing England never hesitates to do for us. The Archbishop is a millstone round Henry Plantagenet's neck. Long live the Archbishop! Anyway, I like the fellow.

SECOND BARON.   My gracious sovereign is master. And so long as our foreign policy permits us to expect nothing of King Henry —

LOUIS.   For the time being, it is an excellent thing to stiffen our attitude. Remember the Montmirail affair. We only signed the peace treaty with Henry on condition that he would spare the lives of the refugees from Brittany and Poitou whom he asked us to hand over to him. Two months later all of them had lost their heads. That directly touched my personal honour. I was not strong enough at the time, so I had to pretend I hadn't heard of these men's execution. And I continued to lavish smiles on my English cousin. But praise God, our affairs have taken a turn for the better. And today *he* needs *us*. So I will now proceed to remember my honour. Show in the ambassadors.

Exit FIRST BARON. *He comes back with* FOLLIOT *and the* DUKE OF ARUNDEL.

FIRST BARON.   Permit me to introduce to your Majesty the two envoys extraordinary from his Highness Henry of England: his Grace the Bishop of London and the Duke of Arundel.

LOUIS (*with a friendly wave to the* DUKE).   Greetings to you, Milord. I have not forgotten your amazing exploits

85

at the last tournament at Calais. Do you still wield a lance as mightily as you did, Milord?

ARUNDEL (*with a gratified bow*).   I hope so, Sire.

LOUIS.   We hope that our friendly relations with your gracious master will allow us to appreciate your jousting skill again before long, on the occasion of the forthcoming festivities.

FOLLIOT *has unrolled a parchment.*

Bishop, I see you have a letter for us from your master. We are listening.

FOLLIOT (*bows again and starts to read*).   'To my Lord and friend Louis, King of the French; Henry, King of England, Duke of Normandy, Duke of Aquitaine and Count of Anjou: Learn that Thomas, former Archbishop of Canterbury, after a public trial held at my court by the plenary assembly of the Barons of my realm has been found guilty of fraud, perjury and treason towards me. He has forthwith fled my kingdom as a traitor, and with evil intent. I therefore entreat you not to allow this criminal, nor any of his adherents, to reside upon your territories, nor to permit any of your vassals to give help, support or counsel to this, my greatest enemy. For I solemnly declare that your enemies or those of your realm would receive none from me or my subjects. I expect you to assist me in the vindication of my honour and the punishment of my enemy, as you would wish me to do for you, should the need arise.'

A pause. FOLLIOT *bows very low and hands the parchment to the* KING, *who rolls it up casually and hands it to one of the* BARONS.

LOUIS.   Gentlemen, we have listened attentively to our gracious cousin's request and we take good note of it.

Our chancellery will draft a reply which will be sent to you tomorrow. All we can do at the moment is express our surprise. No news had reached us of the presence of the Archbishop of Canterbury on our domains.

FOLLIOT (*tersely*). Sire, the former Archbishop has taken refuge at the abbey of St. Martin, near St. Omer.

LOUIS (*still gracious*). My Lord Bishop, we flatter ourselves that there is some order in our kingdom. If he were there, we would certainly have been informed.

> *He makes a gesture of dismissal. The* AMBASSADORS *bow low and go out backwards, ushered out by the* FIRST BARON. *Immediately,* LOUIS *says to the* SECOND BARON.

Show in Thomas Becket and leave us.

> *The* SECOND BARON *goes out and a second later admits* BECKET, *dressed in a monk's robe.* BECKET *drops on to one knee. The* BARON *goes out.*

(*Kindly.*) Rise, Thomas Becket. And greet us as the Primate of England. The bow is enough – and if I know my etiquette, you are entitled to a slight nod of the head from me. There, that's done. I would even be required to kiss your ring, if your visit were an official one. But I have the impression that it isn't. Am I right?

BECKET (*with a smile*). No, Sire. I am only an exile.

LOUIS (*graciously*). That too is an an important title, in France.

BECKET. I am afraid it is the only one I have left. My property has been seized and distributed to those who served the King against me; letters have been sent to the Duke of Flanders and all his barons enjoining them to seize my person. John, Bishop of Poitiers, who was suspected of wanting to grant me asylum, has just been poisoned.

LOUIS (*smiling*).   In fact, you are a very dangerous man.

BECKET.   I'm afraid so.

LOUIS (*unperturbed*).   We like danger, Becket. And if the King of France started being afraid of the King of England, there would be something sadly amiss in Europe. We grant you our royal protection on whichever of our domains it will please you to choose.

BECKET.   I humbly thank your Majesty. I must, however, tell you that I cannot buy this protection with any act hostile to my country.

LOUIS.   You do us injury. That was understood. You may be sure we are practised enough in the task of kingship not to make such gross errors in our choice of spies and traitors. The King of France will ask nothing of you. But. . . . There is always a but, as I'm sure you are aware, in politics.

> BECKET *looks up. The* KING *rises heavily on to his fat legs, goes to him and says familiarly:*

I am only responsible for France's interests, Becket. I really can't afford to shoulder those of heaven. In a month or a year I can summon you back here and tell you just as blandly, that my dealings with the King of England have taken a different turn and that I am obliged to banish you.

> *He slaps him affably on the back, his eyes sparkling with intelligence, and asks, with a smile:*

I believe you have dabbled in politics too, Archbishop?

BECKET (*smiling*).   Yes, Sire. Not so very long ago.

LOUIS (*jovially*).   I like you very much. Mark you, had you been a French bishop, I don't say I wouldn't have clapped you in prison myself. But in the present circumstances, you have a right to my royal protection. Do you value candour, Becket?

BECKET. Yes, Sire.

LOUIS. Then we are sure to understand each other. Do you intend to go and see the Holy Father?

BECKET. Yes, Sire, if you give me your safe conduct.

LOUIS. You shall have it. But a word in your ear, as a friend – keep this to yourself, won't you? Don't go and stir up trouble for me with Rome. – Beware of the Pope. He'll sell you for thirty pieces of silver. The man needs money.

The lights dim. A curtain closes. Two small rostrums, bearing the POPE and the CARDINAL, are pushed on stage, to a light musical accompaniment.

The POPE is a thin, fidgety little man with an atrocious Italian accent. The CARDINAL is swarthy, and his accent is even worse. The whole effect is a little grubby, among the gilded splendour.

POPE. I don't agree, Zambelli! I don't agree at all! It's a very bad plan altogether. We will forfeit our honour all for three thousand silver marks.

CARDINAL. Holy Father, there is no question of forfeiting honour, but merely of taking the sum offered by the King of England and thereby gaining time. To lose that sum and give a negative answer right away would solve neither the problems of the Curia, nor those of Thomas Becket – nor even, I am afraid, those of the higher interests of the Church. To accept the money – the sum is meagre, I agree, and cannot be viewed as a factor in our decision – is merely to make a gesture of appeasement in the interests of peace in Europe. Which has always been the supreme duty of the Holy See.

POPE (*concerned*). If we take money from the King. I cannot possibly receive the Archbishop, who has been

89

waiting here in Rome for a whole month for me to grant
him an audience.

CARDINAL. Receive the money from the King, Very
Holy Father, and receive the Archbishop too. The one
will neutralize the other. The money will remove all sub-
versive taint from the audience you will grant the Archbishop, and on the other hand, the reception of the
Archbishop will efface whatever taint of humiliation
there may have been in accepting the money.

POPE (*gloomily*). I don't want to receive him at all. I
gather he is a sincere man. I am always disconcerted by
people of that sort. They leave me with a bad taste in my
mouth.

CARDINAL. Sincerity is a form of strategy, just like any
other, Holy Father. In certain very difficult negotiations,
when matters are not going ahead and the usual tactics
cease to work, I have been known to use it myself. The
great pitfall, of course, is if your opponent starts being
sincere at the same time as you. Then the game becomes
horribly confusing.

POPE. You know what they say Becket's been meaning to
ask me – in the month he's spent pacing about my ante-
chamber?

CARDINAL (*innocently*). No, Holy Father.

POPE (*impatiently*). Zambelli! Don't play the fox with me!
It was you who told me!

CARDINAL (*caught out*). I beg your pardon, Holy Father,
I had forgotten. Or rather, as your Holiness asked me the
question, I thought you had forgotten and so I took a
chance and —

POPE (*irritably*). Zambelli, if we start out-manoeuvring
each other to no purpose, we'll be here all night!

CARDINAL (*in confusion*). Force of habit, your Holiness.
Excuse me.

90

POPE. To ask me to relieve him of his rank and functions as Archbishop of Canterbury – that's the reason Becket is in Rome! And do you know why he wants to ask me that?

CARDINAL (*candidly for once*). Yes, Holy Father.

POPE (*irritably*). No, you do not know! It was your enemy Rapallo who told me!

CARDINAL (*modestly*). Yes, but I knew it just the same, because I have a spy in Rapallo's palace.

POPE (*with a wink*). Culograti?

CARDINAL. No. Culograti is only my spy in his master's eyes. By the man I have spying on Culograti.

POPE (*cutting short the digression*). Becket maintains that the election of Clarendon was not a free one, that he owes his nomination solely to the royal whim and that consequently the Honour of God, of which he has now decided he is the champion, does not allow him to bear this usurped title any longer. He wishes to be nothing more than an ordinary priest.

CARDINAL (*after a moment's thought*). The man is clearly an abyss of ambition.

POPE. And yet he knows that we know that his title and functions are his only safeguard against the King's anger. I don't give much for his skin, wherever he is, when he is no longer Archbishop!

CARDINAL (*thoughtfully*). He's playing a deep game. But I have a plan. Your Holiness will pretend to believe in his scruples. You will receive him and relieve him of his titles and functions as Primate, then, immediately after, as a reward for his zeal in defending the Church of England, you will re-appoint him Archbishop, in right and due form this time. We thus avert the danger, we score a point against him – and at the same time a point against the King.

POPE.   That's a dangerous game. The King has a long arm.

CARDINAL.   We can cover ourselves. We will send secret letters to the English court explaining that this new nomination is a pure formality and that we herewith rescind the excommunications pronounced by Becket; on the other hand, we will inform Becket of the existence of these secret letters, swearing him to secrecy and begging him to consider them as null and void.

POPE (*getting muddled*).   In that case, perhaps there isn't much point in the letters being secret?

CARDINAL.   Yes, there is. Because that will allow us to manoeuvre with each of them as if the other was ignorant of the contents, while taking the precaution of making it known to them both. The main thing is for them not to know that we know they know. It's so simple a child of twelve could grasp it!

POPE.   But Archbishop or no, what are we going to do with Becket?

CARDINAL (*with a lighthearted wave of his hand*).   We will send him to a convent. A French convent, since King Louis is protecting him – to the Cistercians, say, at Pontigny. The monastic rule is a strict one. It will do that one-time dandy a world of good! Let him learn real poverty! That will teach him to be the comforter of the poor!

POPE.   That sounds like good advice, Zambelli. Bread and water and nocturnal prayers are an excellent remedy for sincerity. (*He muses a moment.*) The only thing that puzzles me, Zambelli, is why you should want to give me a piece of good advice. . . .

The CARDINAL *looks a little embarrassed.*

The little rostra go as they came and the curtain opens revealing a small, bare cell, centre stage.

92

BECKET *is praying before a humble wooden crucifix.*
Crouching in a corner, the LITTLE MONK *is playing*
with a knife.

BECKET. Yet it would be simple enough. Too simple,
perhaps. Saintliness is a temptation too. Oh, how difficult
it is to get an answer from You, Lord! I was slow in praying
to You, but I cannot believe that others, worthier than I,
who have spent years asking You questions, have been
better than myself at deciphering Your real intentions. I
am only a beginner and I must make mistake after mistake, as I did in my Latin translations as a boy, when my
riotous imagination made the old priest roar with
laughter. But I cannot believe that one learns Your lan-
guage as one learns any human tongue, by hard studying,
with a dictionary, a grammar and a set of idioms. I am
sure that to the hardened sinner, who drops to his knees for
the first time and murmurs Your name, marvelling, You tell
Your secrets, straight away, and that he understands. I have
served You like a dilettante, surprised that I could still
find my pleasure in Your service. And for a long time I was
on my guard because of it. I could not believe this pleasure
would bring me one step nearer to You. I could not believe
that the road could be a happy one. Their hairshirts, their
fasting, their bells in the small hours summoning us to
meet You, on the icy paving-stones, in the sick misery of the
poor ill-treated human animal – I cannot believe that all
these are anything but safeguards for the weak. In power
and in luxury, and even in the pleasures of the flesh, I
shall not cease to speak to You, I feel this now. You are
the God of the rich man and the happy man too, Lord,
and therein lies Your profound justice. You do not turn
away Your eyes from the man who has been given everything from birth. You have not abandoned him, alone in

his ensnaring ease. And he may be Your true lost sheep. For Your scheme of things, which we mistakenly call justice, is secret and profound and You plumb the hidden depths of poor men's puny frames as carefully as those of kings. And beneath those outward differences, which blind us, but which to You are barely noticeable, beneath the diadem or the grime, You discern the same pride, the same vanity, the same petty, complacent preoccupation with oneself. Lord, I am certain now that You meant to tempt me with this hairshirt, object of so much vapid self-congratulation! This bare cell, this solitude, this absurdly endured winter-cold – and the conveniences of prayer. It would be too easy to buy You like this, at so low a price. I shall leave this convent, where so many precautions hem You round. I shall take up the mitre and the golden cope again, and the great silver cross, and I shall go back and fight in the place and with the weapons it has pleased You to give me. It has pleased You to make me Archbishop and to set me, like a solitary pawn, face to face with the king, upon the chessboard. I shall go back to my place, humbly, and let the world accuse me of pride, so that I may do what I believe is my life's work. For the rest, Your will be done.

He crosses himself.

The LITTLE MONK *is still playing with his knife. Suddenly he throws it and watches as it quivers, embedded in the floor.*

CURTAIN

ACT FOUR

The King of France's Court.

> KING LOUIS *comes in, holding* BECKET *familiarly by the arm.*

LOUIS. I tell you, Becket, intrigue is an ugly thing. You keep the smell about you for ages afterwards. There is a return of good understanding between the kingdom of England and ourselves. Peace in that direction assures me of a great advantage in the struggle which I will shortly have to undertake against the Emperor. I must protect my rear by a truce with Henry Plantagenet, before I march towards the east. And, needless to say, you are one of the items on the King's bill of charges. I can even tell you that apart from yourself, his demands are negligible. (*Musingly.*) Curious man. England's best policy would have been to take advantage of the Emperor's aggressive intentions and close the other jaw of the trap. He is deliberately sacrificing this opportunity for the pleasure of seeing you driven out. He really hates you, doesn't he?

BECKET (*simply*). Sire, we loved each other and I think he cannot forgive me for preferring God to him.

LOUIS. Your King isn't doing his job properly, Archbishop. He is giving way to passion. However! He has chosen to score a point against you, instead of against me. You are on his bill; I have to pay his price and banish you. I do not do so without a certain shame. Where are you thinking of going?

BECKET. I am a shepherd who has remained too long

95

away from his flock. I intend to go back to England. I had already made my decision before this audience with your Majesty.

LOUIS (*surprised*).   You have a taste for martyrdom? You disappoint me. I thought you more healthy-minded.

BECKET.   Would it be healthy-minded to walk the roads of Europe, and beg a refuge where my carcass would be safe? Besides, where would I be safe? I am Primate of England. That is a rather showy label on my back. The honour of God and common sense, which for once coincide, dictate that instead of risking the knife thrust of some hired assassin, on the highway, I should go and have myself killed – if killed I must be – clad in my golden cope, with my mitre on my head and my silver cross in my hand, among my flock in my own cathedral. That place alone befits me.

A pause.

LOUIS.   I dare say you're right. (*He sighs.*) Ah, what a pity it is to be a king, sometimes, when one has the surprise of meeting a man! You'll tell me, fortunately for me, that men are rare. Why weren't you born on this side of the Channel, Becket? (*He smiles.*) True, you would no doubt have been a thorn in *my* side then! The honour of God is a very cumbersome thing. (*He muses for a moment and then says abruptly.*) Who cares, I'll risk it! I like you too much. I'll indulge in a moment's humanity. I am going to try something, even if your master does seize on the chance to double his bill. After all, banishing you would merely have cost me a small slice of honour. . . . I am meeting Henry in a day or two, at La Ferté Bernard, to seal our agreement. I shall try to persuade him to make his peace with you. Should he agree, will you be willing to talk with him?

BECKET. Sire, ever since we stopped seeing each other, I have never ceased to talk to him.

Blackout. Prolonged blare of trumpets. The set is completely removed. Nothing remains but the cyclorama around the bare stage. A vast, arid plain, lashed by the wind. Trumpets again.

Two SENTRIES *are on stage, watching something in the distance.*

SENTRY. Open those eyes of yours, lad! And drink it all in. You're new to the job, but you won't see something like this every day! This is a historic meeting!

YOUNG SENTRY. I dare say, but it's perishing cold! How long are they going to keep us hanging about?

SENTRY. We're sheltered by the wood here, but you can bet they're even colder than we are, out there on the plain.

YOUNG SENTRY. Look! They've come up to each other! I wonder what they're talking about?

SENTRY. What do you think they're talking about, muttonhead? Inquiring how things are at home? Complaining about their chilblains? The fate of the world, that's what they're arguing about! Things you and I won't ever understand. Even the words those bigwigs use – why, you wouldn't even know what they meant!

They go off. The lights go up. BECKET *and the* KING, *on horseback, are alone in the middle of the plain, facing each other.*

Throughout the scene, the winter blizzard wails like a shrill dirge beneath their words. And during their silences, only the wind is heard.

KING. You look older, Thomas.

BECKET. You too, Highness. Are you sure you aren't too cold?

KING.   I'm frozen stiff. You love it of course! You're in your element, aren't you? And you're barefooted as well!

BECKET (*smiling*).   That's my latest affectation.

KING.   Even with these fur boots on, my chilblains are killing me. Aren't yours, or don't you have any?

BECKET (*gently*).   Of course.

KING (*cackling*).   You're offering them up to God, I hope, holy monk?

BECKET (*gravely*).   I have better things to offer Him.

KING (*with a sudden cry*).   If we start straight away, we're sure to quarrel! Let's talk about trivial things. You know my son is fourteen? He's come of age.

BECKET.   Has he improved at all?

KING.   He's a little idiot and sly like his mother. Becket, don't you ever marry!

BECKET (*smiling*).   The matter has been taken out of my hands. By your Highness! It was you who had me ordained!

KING (*with a cry*).   Let's not start yet, I tell you! Talk about something else!

BECKET (*lightly*).   Has your Highness done much hunting lately?

KING (*snarling*).   Yes, every day! And it doesn't amuse me any more.

BECKET.   Have you any new hawks?

KING (*furiously*).   The most expensive on the market! But they don't fly straight.

BECKET.   And your horses?

KING.   The Sultan sent me four superb stallions for the tenth anniversary of my reign. But they throw everyone! Nobody has managed to mount one of them yet!

BECKET (*smiling*).   I must see what I can do about that some day.

KING.   They'll throw you too! And we'll see your buttocks

98

under your robe! At least, I hope so, or everything would be too dismal.

BECKET (*after a pause*). Do you know what I miss most, Sire? The horses.

KING. And the women?

BECKET (*simply*). I've forgotten.

KING. You hypocrite. You turned into a hypocrite when you became a priest. (*Abruptly.*) Did you love Gwendolen?

BECKET. I've forgotten her too.

KING. You did love her! That's the only way I can account for it.

BECKET (*gravely*). No, my prince, in my soul and conscience, I did not love her.

KING. Then you never loved anything, that's worse! (*Churlishly.*) Why are you calling me your prince, as in the old days?

BECKET (*gently*). Because you have remained my prince.

KING (*crying out*). Then why are you doing me harm?

BECKET (*gently*). Let's talk about something else.

KING. Well, what? I'm cold.

BECKET. I always told you, my prince, that one must fight the cold with the cold's own weapons. Strip naked and splash yourself with cold water every morning.

KING. I used to when you were there to force me into it. I never wash now. I stink. I grew a beard at one time. Did you know?

BECKET (*smiling*). Yes. I had a hearty laugh over it.

KING. I cut it off because it itched. (*He cries out suddenly, like a lost child.*) Becket, I'm bored!

BECKET (*gravely*). My prince, I do so wish I could help you.

KING. Then what are you waiting for? You can see I'm dying for it!

BECKET (*quietly*).   I'm waiting for the honour of God and the honour of the King to become one.

KING.   You'll wait a long time then!

BECKET.   Yes, I'm afraid I will.

A pause. Only the wind is heard.

KING (*suddenly*).   If we've nothing more to say to each other, we might as well go and get warm!

BECKET.   We have everything to say to each other, my prince. The opportunity may not occur again.

KING.   Make haste, then. Or there'll be two frozen statues on this plain, making their peace in a frozen eternity! I am your King, Becket! And so long as we are on this earth you owe me the first move! I'm prepared to forget a lot of things but not the fact that I am King. You yourself taught me that.

BECKET (*gravely*).   Never forget it, my prince. Even against God. You have a different task to do. You have to steer the ship.

KING.   And you—what do you have to do?

BECKET.   Resist you with all my might, when you steer against the wind.

KING.   Do you expect the wind to be behind me, Becket? No such luck! That's fairy tale navigation! God on the King's side? That's never happened yet! Yes, once in a century, at the time of the Crusades, when all Christendom shouts 'It's God's will!' And even then! You know as well as I do what private greeds a Crusade covers up, in nine cases out of ten. The rest of the time it's a head-on wind. And there must be somebody to keep the watch!

BECKET.   And somebody else to cope with the absurd wind and with God. The tasks have been shared out, once

100

and for all. The pity of it is that it should have been between us two, my prince – who were friends.

KING (*crossly*). The King of France – I still don't know what he hopes to gain by it – preached at me for three whole days for me to make my peace with you. What good would it do you to provoke me beyond endurance?

BECKET. None.

KING. You know that I am the King, and that I must act like a King! What do you expect of me? Are you hoping I'll weaken?

BECKET. No That would prostrate me.

KING. Do you hope to conquer me by force, then?

BECKET. You are the strong one.

KING. To win me round?

BECKET. No. Not that either. It is not for me to win you round. I have only to say no to you.

KING. But you must be logical, Becket!

BECKET. No. That isn't necessary, my liege. We must only do – absurdly – what we have been given to do – right to the end.

KING. Yet I know you well enough, God knows. Ten years we spent together, little Saxon! At the hunt, at the whorehouse, at war; carousing all night long, the two of us; in the same girl's bed, sometimes . . . and at work in the council chamber too. Absurdly. . . . That word isn't like you.

BECKET. Perhaps. I am no longer like myself.

KING (*derisively*). Have you been touched by grace?

BECKET (*gravely*). Not by the one you think. I am not worthy of it.

KING. Did you feel the Saxon in you coming out, despite papa's good collaborator's sentiments?

BECKET. No. Not that either.

KING. What then?

BECKET.   I felt for the first time that I was being entrusted
with something, that's all – there in that empty cathedral,
somewhere in France, that day when you ordered me to
take up this burden. I was a man without honour. And
suddenly I found it – one I never imagined would ever
become mine – the Honour of God. A frail, incompre-
hensible honour, vulnerable as a boy-king fleeing from
danger.

KING (*roughly*).   Suppose we talked a little more precisely,
Becket, with words I understand? Otherwise we'll be here
all night. I'm cold. And the others are waiting for us on
the fringes of this plain.

BECKET.   I am being precise.

KING.   I'm an idiot then! Talk to me like an idiot! That's
an order. Will you lift the excommunication which you
pronounced on William of Aynesford and others of my
liegemen?

BECKET.   No, Sire, because that is the only weapon I have
to defend this child, who was given, naked, into my care.

KING.   Will you agree to the twelve proposals which my
bishops have accepted in your absence at Northampton,
and notably to forgo the much abused protection of
Saxon clerics who get themselves tonsured to escape land
bondage?

BECKET.   No, Sire. My role is to defend my sheep. And
they are my sheep. (*A pause.*) Nor will I concede that the
bishops should forgo the right to appoint priests in their
own dioceses, nor that churchmen should be subject to any
but the Church's jurisdiction. These are my duties as a
pastor – which it is not for me to relinquish. But I shall
agree to the nine other articles in a spirit of peace, and
because I know that you must remain King – in all save
the honour of God.

   A pause.

102

KING (*coldly*).   Very well. I will help you defend your God, since that is your new vocation, in memory of the companion you once were to me – in all save the honour of the realm. You may come back to England, Thomas.

BECKET.   Thank you, my prince. I meant to go back in any case and give myself up to your power, for on this earth, you are my King. And in all that concerns this earth, I owe you obedience.

A pause.

KING (*ill at ease*).   Well, let's go back now. We've finished. I'm cold.

BECKET (*dully*).   I feel cold too, now.

Another pause. They look at each other. The wind howls.

KING (*suddenly*).   You never loved me, did you, Becket?

BECKET.   In so far as I was capable of love, yes, my prince, I did.

KING.   Did you start to love God? (*He cries out.*) You mule! Can't you ever answer a simple question?

BECKET (*quietly*).   I started to love the honour of God.

KING (*sombrely*).   Come back to England. I give you my royal peace. May you find yours. And may you not discover you were wrong about yourself. This is the last time I shall come begging to you. (*He cries out.*) I should never have seen you again! It hurts too much. (*His whole body is suddenly shaken by a sob.*)

BECKET (*goes nearer to him, moved*).   My prince —

KING (*yelling*).   No! No pity! It's dirty. Stand away from me! Go back to England! It's too cold out here!

BECKET turns his horse and moves nearer to the KING.

BECKET (*gravely*).   Farewell, my prince. Will you give me the kiss of peace?

103

KING. No! I can't bear to come near you! I can't bear to look at you! Later! Later! When it doesn't hurt any more!

BECKET. I shall set sail tomorrow. Farewell, my prince. I know I shall never see you again.

KING (*his face twisted with hatred*). How dare you say that to me after I gave you my royal word? Do you take me for a traitor?

BECKET *looks at him gravely for a second longer, with a sort of pity in his eyes. Then he slowly turns his horse and rides away. The wind howls.*

KING. Thomas!

But BECKET *has not heard. The* KING *does not call a second time. He spurs his horse and gallops off in the other direction. The lights fade. The wind howls.*

The lights change. Red curtains fall. BECKET'S *whistled march is heard offstage during the scene change.*

The curtains open. Royal music. KING HENRY'S *palace somewhere in France. The two* QUEENS, *the* BARONS *and* HENRY'S SON *are standing round the dinner table, waiting. The* KING, *his eyes gleaming maliciously, looks at them and then exclaims:*

KING. Today, gentlemen, I shall not be the first to sit down! (*To his* SON, *with a comic bow.*) You are the King, Sir. The honour belongs to you. Take the high chair. Today I shall wait on *you!*

QUEEN MOTHER (*with slight irritation*). My son!

KING. I know what I'm doing, Madam! (*With a sudden shout.*) Go on, you great loon, look sharp! You're the King, but you're as stupid as ever!

His SON *flinches to avoid the blow he was expecting and goes to sit in the* KING'S *chair, sly and rather ill at ease.*

Take your places, gentlemen! I shall remain standing. Barons of England, here is your second King. For the good of our vast domains, a kingly colleague had become a necessity. Reviving an ancient custom, we have decided to have our successor crowned during our lifetime and to share our responsibilities with him. We ask you now to give him your homage and to honour him with the same title as ourself.

He makes a sign. Two SERVANTS *have brought in a haunch of venison on a silver charger. The* KING *serves his* SON.

YOUNG QUEEN (*to her* SON). Sit up straight! And try to eat properly for once, now that you've been raised to glory!

KING (*grunting as he serves him*). He hasn't the face for it! He's a little slyboots and dimwitted at that. However, he'll be our King in good earnest one day, so you may as well get used to him. Besides, it's the best I had to offer.

QUEEN MOTHER (*indignantly*). Really, my son! This game is unworthy of you and of us. You insisted on it – against my advice. At least play it with dignity!

KING (*rounding on her in fury*). I'll play the games that amuse me, Madam, and I'll play them the way I choose! This mummery, gentlemen, which is, incidentally, without any importance at all – if your new King fidgets, let me know, I'll give him a good kick up his train – will at the very least have the appreciable result of showing our new friend the Archbishop that we can do without him. If

105

there was one ancient privilege the Primacy clung to, tooth and nail, it was its exclusive right to anoint and consecrate the Kings of this realm. Well, it will be that old toad the Archbishop of York – with letters from the Pope authorizing him to do so – I paid the price! – who, tomorrow, will crown our son in the cathedral! What a joke that's going to be! (*He roars with laughter amid the general silence.*) What a tremendous, marvellous joke! I'd give anything to see the Archbishop's face when he has to swallow that! (*To his* SON.) Get down from there, you imbecile! Go back to the bottom of the table and take your victuals with you! You aren't officially crowned until tomorrow.

> His SON *picks up his plate and goes back to his place, casting a cowed, smouldering look at his father.*

(*Watching him, he says jovially.*) What a look! Filial sentiments are a fine thing to see, gentlemen! You'd like to be the real King wouldn't you, you young pig? You'd like that number III after your name, eh, with Papa good and stiff under his catafalque! You'll have to wait a bit! Papa is well. Papa is very well indeed!

QUEEN MOTHER.   My son, God knows I criticized your attempts at reconciliation with that wretch, who has done us nothing but harm . . . God knows I understand your hatred of him! But do not let it drag you into making a gesture you will regret, merely for the sake of wounding his pride. Henry is still a child. But you were not much older when you insisted on reigning by yourself, and in opposition to me. Ambitious self-seekers – and there is never any scarcity of those around princes – can advise him, raise a faction against you and avail themselves of this hasty coronation to divide the kingdom! Think it over; there is still time.

KING. We are still alive, Madam, and in control! And nothing can equal my pleasure in imagining my proud friend Becket's face when he sees the fundamental privilege of the Primacy whisked from under his nose! I let him cheat me out of one or two articles the other day, but I had something up my sleeve for him!

QUEEN MOTHER. Henry! I bore the weight of state affairs longer than you ever have. I have been your queen and I am your mother. You are answerable for the interests of a great Kingdom, not for your moods. You already gave far too much away to the King of France, at La Ferté Bernard. It is England you must think of, not your hatred – or disappointed love – for that man.

KING (*in a fury*). Disappointed love – disappointed love? What gives you the right, Madam, to meddle in my loves and hates?

QUEEN MOTHER. You have a rancour against the man which is neither healthy or manly. The King your father dealt with his enemies faster and more summarily than that. He had them killed and said no more about it. If Thomas Becket were a faithless woman whom you still hankered after, you would act no differently. Sweet Jesu, tear him out of your heart once and for all! (*She bawls suddenly.*) Oh, if I were a man!

KING (*grinning*). Thanks be to God, Madam, he gave you dugs. Which I never personally benefited from. I was suckled by a peasant girl.

QUEEN MOTHER (*acidly*). That is no doubt why you have remained so lumpish, my son.

QUEEN. And haven't I a say in the matter? I tolerated your mistresses, Sir, but do you expect me to tolerate everything? Have you ever stopped to think what kind of woman I am? I am tired of having my life encumbered with this man. Becket! Always Becket! Nobody ever talks

107

about anything else here! He was almost less of a hindrance when you loved him. I am a woman. I am your wife and your queen. I refuse to be treated like this! I shall complain to my father, the Duke of Aquitaine! I shall complain to my uncle the Emperor! I shall complain to all the Kings of Europe, my cousins! I shall complain to God!

KING (*shouting rather vulgarly*). I should start with God! Be off to your private chapel, Madam, and see if he's at home. (*He turns to his mother, fuming.*) And you, the other Madam, away to your chamber with your secret councillors and go and spin your webs! Get out, both of you! I can't stand the sight of you! I retch with boredom whenever I set eyes on you! And young Henry III too! Go on, get out! (*He chases him out with kicks, yelling.*) Here's my royal foot in your royal buttocks! And to the devil with my whole family, if he'll have you! Get out, all of you! Get out! Get out! Get out!

The QUEENS *scurry out, with a great rustling of silks.*

He turns go the BARONS, *who all stand watching him, terror-stricken.*

(*More calmly.*) Let us drink, gentlemen. That's about all one can do in your company, Let us get drunk, like men, all night; until we roll under the table, in vomit and oblivion.

He fills their glasses and beckons them closer.

Ah, my four idiots! My beautiful hounds! It's warm beside you, like being in a stable. Good sweat! Comfortable nothingness! (*He taps their skulls.*) Not the least little glimmer inside to spoil the fun. And to think that before he came I was like you! A good fat machine for belching after drink, for pissing, for mounting girls and punching heads. What the devil did you put into it, Becket, to stop the wheels from going round? (*Suddenly to a* BARON.) Tell me, do you think sometimes, Baron?

SECOND BARON. Never, Sire. Thinking has never agreed with an Englishman. It's unhealthy. Besides, a gentleman has better things to do.

KING (*sitting beside them, suddenly quite calm*). Drink up gentlemen. That's always been considered a healthy thing to do. (*He fills the goblets.*) Has Becket landed? I'm told the sea has been too rough to cross these last few days.

FIRST BARON (*sombrely*). He has landed, Sire, despite the sea.

KING. Where?

FIRST BARON. On a deserted stretch of coast, near Sandwich.

KING. So God did not choose to drown him?

FIRST BARON. No.

KING (*he asks in his sly, brutish way*). Was nobody there waiting for him? There must be one or two men in England whom he can't call his friends!

FIRST BARON. Yes, Gervase, Duke of Kent, Regnouf de Broc and Regnault de Garenne were waiting for him. Gervase had said that if he dared to land he'd cut off his head with his own hands. But the native Englishmen from all the coastal towns had armed themselves to form an escort for the Archbishop. And the Dean of Oxford went to meet the barons and charged them not to cause bloodshed and make you look a traitor, seeing that you had given the Archbishop a safe conduct.

KING (*soberly*). Yes, I gave him a safe conduct.

FIRST BARON. All along the road to Canterbury, the peasants, the artisans and the small shopkeepers came out to meet him, cheering him and escorting him from village to village. Not a single rich man, not a single Norman showed his face.

109

KING. Only the Saxons?

FIRST BARON. Poor people armed with makeshift shields and rusty lances. Riff-raff. Swarms of them, though, all camping around Canterbury, to protect him. (*Gloomily.*) Who would have thought there were so many people in England!

The KING *has remained prostrate without uttering a word. Now he suddenly jumps up and roars:*

KING. A miserable wretch who ate my bread! A man I raised up from nothing! A Saxon! A man I loved! (*Shouting like a madman.*) I loved him! Yes, I loved him! And I believe I still do! Enough, O God! Enough! Stop, stop, O God, I've had enough!

He flings himself down on the couch, sobbing hysterically; tearing at the horse-hair mattress with his teeth, and eating it. The BARONS, *stupefied, go nearer to him.*

FIRST BARON (*timidly*). Your Highness. . . .

KING (*moaning, with his head buried in the mattress*). I can do nothing! Nothing! I'm as limp and useless as a girl! So long as he's alive, I'll never be able to do a thing. I tremble before him astonished. And I am the King! (*With a sudden cry.*) Will no one rid me of him? A priest! A priest who jeers at me and does me injury! Are there none but cowards like myself around me? Are there no men left in England? Oh, my heart! My heart is beating too fast to bear!

He lies, still as death on the torn mattress. The four BARONS *stand around speechless. Suddenly, on a percussion instrument, there rises a rhythmic beating, a sort of muffled tom-tom which is at first only the agitated heartbeats of the* KING, *but which swells and grows more insistent. The four* BARONS *look at each other. Then they straighten, buckle their swordbelts, pick up their helmets and go slowly out, leaving the* KING *alone with the muffled rhythm of the heartbeats, which will continue until the murder. The* KING *lies there prostrate, among the upturned benches, in the deserted hall. A torch splutters and goes out. He sits up, looks around, sees they have gone, and suddenly realizes why. A wild, lost look comes into his eyes. A moment's pause, then he collapses on the bed with a long broken moan.*

KING.   O my Thomas!

A second torch goes out. Total darkness. Only the steady throb of the heartbeats is heard. A dim light. The forest of pillars again. Canterbury cathedral. Upstage a small altar, with three steps leading up to it, half screened by a grill. In a corner downstage BECKET *and the* LITTLE MONK, *who is helping him on with his vestments. Near by, on a stool, the Archbishop's mitre. The tall silver cross is leaning against a pillar.*

BECKET.   I must look my best today. Make haste.

The LITTLE MONK *fumbles with the vestments. The muffled tom-tom is heard distantly at first, then closer.*

LITTLE MONK.   It's difficult with all those little laces. It wants a girl's hands.

BECKET (*softly*).   A man's hands are better, today. Never mind the laces. The alb, quickly. And the stole. And then the cope.

LITTLE MONK (*conscientiously*).   If it's worth doing it's worth doing well.

BECKET.   You're quite right. If it's worth doing it's worth

doing well. Do up all the little laces, every one of them.
God will give us time.

A pause. The LITTLE MONK *struggles manfully on,
putting out his tongue in concentration. The throbbing
grows louder.*

(*Smiling.*) Don't pull your tongue out like that! (*He
watches the* LITTLE MONK *as he works away.*)

LITTLE MONK (*sweating but content*).   There. That's all
done. But I'd rather have cleaned out our pigsty at home!
It's not half such hard work!

BECKET.   Now the alb. (*A pause.*) Were you fond of your
pigs?

LITTLE MONK (*his eyes lighting up*).   Yes, I was.

BECKET.   At my father's house, we had some pigs too,
when I was a child. (*Smiling.*) We're two rough lads from
Hastings, you and I! Give me the chasuble.

BECKET *kisses the chasuble and slips it over his head.
He looks at the* LITTLE MONK *and says gently:*

Do you miss your knife?

LITTLE MONK.   Yes. (*Pause.*) Will it be today?

BECKET (*gravely*).   I think so, my son. Are you afraid?

LITTLE MONK.   Oh, no. Not if we have time to fight.
All I want is the chance to strike a few blows first; so I
shan't have done nothing but receive them all my life. If
I can kill one Norman first – just one, I don't want much
– one for one, that will seem fair and right enough to
me.

BECKET (*with a kindly smile*).   Are you so very set on
killing one?

LITTLE MONK.   One for one. After that, I don't much
care if I *am* just a little grain of sand in the machine.
Because I know that by putting more and more grains of

sand in the machine, one day it will come grinding to a
stop.

BECKET (*gently*).   And on that day, what then?

LITTLE MONK.   We'll set a fine, new, well-oiled machine
in the place of the old one and this time we'll put the
Normans into it instead. (*He asks, quite without irony.*)
That's what justice means, isn't it?

BECKET *smiles and does not answer him.*

BECKET.   Fetch me the mitre. (*He says quietly, as the*
LITTLE MONK *fetches it.*) O Lord, You forbade Peter to
strike a blow in the Garden of Olives. But I shall not
deprive him of that joy. He has had too few joys in his
short span on earth. (*To the* LITTLE MONK.) Now give
me my silver cross. I must hold it.

LITTLE MONK (*passing it to him*).   Lord, it's heavy! A
good swipe with that and they'd feel it! My word, I wish
I could have it!

BECKET (*stroking his hair*).   Lucky little Saxon! This black
world will have been in order to the end, for you. (*He
straightens, grave once more.*) There, I'm ready, all
adorned for Your festivities, Lord. Do not, in this interval
of waiting, let one last doubt enter my soul.

*During this scene, the throbbing has grown louder. Now
it mingles with a loud knocking on the door. A* PRIEST
runs in wildly.

PRIEST.   Your Grace! There are four armed men outside!
They say they must see you on behalf of the King. I've
barricaded the door but they're breaking it in! They've
got hatchets! Quickly! You must go into the back of the
church and have the choir gates closed! They're strong
enough, they'll hold!

BECKET (*calmly*).   It is time for vespers, William. Does

113

one close the choir gates during vespers? I never heard of such a thing.

PRIEST (*nonplussed*).   I know, but. . . .

BECKET.   Everything must be the way it should be. The choir gates will remain open. Come, boy, let us go up to the altar. This is no place to be.

> *He goes towards the altar, followed by the* LITTLE MONK. *A great crash. The door has given way. The four* BARONS *come in, in their helmets. They fling down their hatchets and draw their swords.* BECKET *turns to face them, grave and calm, at the foot of the altar. They stop a moment, uncertain and disconcerted; four statues huge and threatening. The tom-tom has stopped. There is nothing now but a heavy silence.* BECKET *says simply:*

Here it comes. The supreme folly. This is its hour.

> *He holds their eyes. They dare not move. He says coldly:*

One does not enter armed into God's house. What do you want?

FIRST BARON (*thickly*).   Your death.

> *A pause.*

SECOND BARON (*thickly*).   You bring shame to the King. Flee the country or you're a dead man.

BECKET (*softly*).   It is time for the service.

> *He turns to the altar and faces the tall crucifix without paying any further attention to them. The throbbing starts again, muffled. The four* BARONS *close in like automata. The* LITTLE MONK *suddenly leaps forward brandishing the heavy silver cross in order to protect* BECKET, *but one of the* BARONS *swings his sword and*

114

fells him to the ground. BECKET *murmurs, as if in reproach.*

Not even one! It would have given him so much pleasure, Lord. (*With a sudden cry.*) Oh, how difficult you make it all! And how heavy your honour is to bear! (*He adds, very quietly.*) Poor Henry.

The four BARONS *hurl themselves on to him. He falls at the first blow. They hack at his body, grunting like woodcutters. The* PRIEST *has fled with a long scream, which echoes in the empty cathedral.*
Blackout.

On the same spot. The KING, *naked, on bended knees at* BECKET'S *tomb, as in the first scene. Four* MONKS *are whipping him with ropes, almost duplicating the gestures of the* BARONS *as they killed* BECKET.

KING (*crying out*). Are you satisfied now, Becket? Does this settle our account? Has the honour of God been washed clean?

The four MONKS *finish beating him, then kneel down and bow their heads. The* KING *mutters – one feels it is part of the ceremony.*

Thank you. Yes, yes, of course, it was agreed, I forgive you. Many thanks.

The PAGE *comes forward with a vast cloak, which the* KING *wraps round himself. The* BARONS *surround the* KING *and help him to dress, while the* BISHOPS *and the* CLERGY, *forming a procession, move away solemnly upstage to the strains of the organ. The* KING *dresses hurriedly, with evident bad temper, aided by his* BARONS. *He grimaces illhumouredly and growls:*

115

The pigs! The Norman bishops just went through the motions, but those little Saxon monks – my word, they had their money's worth!

A BARON *comes in. A joyful peal of bells is heard.*

BARON. Sire, the operation has been successful! The Saxon mob is yelling with enthusiasm outside the cathedral, acclaiming your Majesty's name in the same breath as Becket's! If the Saxons are on our side now, Prince Henry's followers look as though they have definitely lost the day.

KING (*with a touch of hypocritical majesty beneath his slightly loutish manner*). The honour of God, gentlemen, is a very good thing, and taken all in all, one gains by having it on one's side. Thomas Becket, who was our friend, used to say so. England will owe her ultimate victory over chaos to him, and it is our wish that, henceforward, he should be honoured and prayed to in this kingdom as a saint. Come, gentlemen. We will determine, tonight, in Council, what posthumous honours to render him and what punishment to deal out to his murderers.

FIRST BARON (*imperturbably*). Sire, they are unknown.

KING (*impenetrably*). Our justice will seek them out, Baron, and you will be specially entrusted with this inquiry, so that no one will be in any doubt as to our royal desire to defend the honour of God and the memory of our friend from this day forward.

The organ swells triumphantly, mingled with the sound of the bells and the cheering of the crowds as they file out.

CURTAIN

Methuen's Modern Plays